TOP **10**
LAS VEGAS

CONNIE EMERSON

EYEWITNESS TRAVEL

Left **Bellagio** Center **The Forum Shops at Caesars** Right **The Venetian**

DK

LONDON, NEW YORK,
MELBOURNE, MUNICH AND DELHI
www.dk.com

Produced by
Blue Island Publishing, London

Reproduced by Colourscan, Singapore
Printed and bound by South China Printing
Co. Ltd, China

First published in Great Britain in 2002 by
Dorling Kindersley Limited
80 Strand, London WC2R 0RL
A Penguin Company

**Reprinted with revisions 2003, 2005,
2007, 2009**

**Copyright 2002, 2009 © Dorling
Kindersley Limited, London**

A CIP catalogue record is available from the
British Library.

ISBN: 978 1 40533 477 8

Within each Top 10 list in this book,
no hierarchy of quality or popularity is implied. All 10
are, in the editors' opinion, of roughly equal merit.

Floors are referred to thoughtout in accordance
with American usage; ie the "first floor" is at
ground level.

MIX
Paper from
responsible sources
FSC™ C018179
www.fsc.org

Contents

Las Vegas Top 10

The information in this DK Eyewitness Top 10 Travel Guide is checked regularly.
Every effort has been made to ensure that this book is as up-to-date as possible at the time of
going to press. Some details, however, such as telephone numbers, opening hours, prices,
gallery hanging arrangements and travel information are liable to change. The publishers
cannot accept responsibility for any consequences arising from the use of this book, nor for
any material on third party websites, and cannot guarantee that any website address in this
book will be a suitable source of travel information. We value the views and suggestions of
our readers very highly. Please write to: Publisher, DK Eyewitness Travel Guides,
Dorling Kindersley, 80 Strand, London, Great Britain WC2R 0RL.

Left **Golden Nugget Casino** Center left **Jubilee** Center right **Wedding chapel** Right **Legacy Golf**

Left **Fremont Street Experience** Right **Grand Canyon**

Following pages **Vegas Vic, Glitter Gulch**

LAS VEGAS
TOP 10

LAS VEGAS TOP 10

❿ Las Vegas Highlights

The Entertainment Capital of the World offers just about everything: the world's largest hotels; the brightest stars in show business; shops and restaurants that rival any on earth. It's true, too, that the lights are brighter in Las Vegas. Yet you don't have to go far from the glamour and glitter to find the natural beauty of lakes and the desert as well.

The Strip
The neon artery of gambling pulses with excitement. Imaginatively themed resorts make it a street that never sleeps *(see pp8–9).*

Hoover Dam
An engineering marvel, the dam not only tamed the raging Colorado River but also created the enormous Lake Mead, providing myriad aquatic pursuits, just minutes from the Las Vegas city limits *(see pp10–11).*

Glitter Gulch
The heart of Las Vegas in its early days, downtown's centerpiece, Glitter Gulch, experienced a rebirth in the late 1990s *(see pp12–13).*

Bellagio
The hotel that upped the ante as far as Las Vegas luxury is concerned. It is well located, too *(see pp14–15).*

The Venetian
The Italian Renaissance revisited. Minstrels and nobility stroll among the Venetian landmarks; gondoliers glide by *(see pp20–21)*.

Grand Canyon
The ultimate excursion from Las Vegas. Whether their trip is by airplane, bus, or automobile, most visitors say the experience is unforgettable *(see pp16–19)*.

Wynn Las Vegas
This opulent megaresort is set in beautiful landscaped gardens *(see pp22–3)*.

Red Rock Canyon
Not far from the city lights, this escarpment shimmers in the setting sun *(see pp24–5)*.

The Forum Shops at Caesars
The glory that was Rome provides the backdrop for a choice of upscale shops and restaurants *(see pp26–7)*.

Madame Tussaud's Wax Museum
Rub shoulders with the stars of the entertainment and sporting worlds, and learn how wax reproductions look so very real *(see pp28–9)*.

🔟 The Strip

Nowhere are the glitz and glitter of Las Vegas, or its ambivalence, so apparent as along the Strip. This 4-mile (6-km) long thoroughfare (actually a section of Las Vegas Boulevard) is the entertainment capital of the world and home to many of the largest hotels and casinos on the planet. The extravaganza of both its adult entertainment and family favorites makes Las Vegas a city of superlatives. The Strip is a master of reinvention, selling itself on seemingly contradictory values: hedonism one decade, family fun the next.

The Strip by day

Top 10 Sights

1. The Strip by Night
2. The Strip by Day
3. Older Hotel-Casinos
4. Theme Casinos
5. The Five Megaresorts
6. Fashion Show Mall
7. The Forum Shops at Caesars
8. Hole-in-the-Wall Businesses
9. Hawaiian Marketplace
10. Impersonators

🅞 You're on vacation – why *not* have doughnuts for breakfast?! Delicious "Krispy Kreme" doughnuts are on sale at Excalibur, at the entrance to TI, and in other Strip casinos.

🕑 To experience the excitement fully, get a hotel room with a view of the Strip. Best of all are the upper floors of the Venetian or TI, facing south.

Put on your shopping shoes early to beat the crowds at stores along the Strip. Or else patronize the hotel shops, which stay open until late.

• Map M3–R2 • General information: Las Vegas Convention and Visitors Authority • 3150 Paradise Road • 702 892 0711 or 1877 847 4858 • www.visitlasvegas. com

The Strip by Night

After dark is when the Strip is meant to be seen: its miles of neon tubes, millions of twinkling, pulsing, flashing lights, vast fiber-optic signs, and, of course, thousands of people create an almost euphoric excitement.

The Strip by Day

Although daytime lacks the glitter of the night, the Strip starts coming to life from mid-morning, when the street and sidewalks become thronged with cars and pedestrians. The Strip is one of 15 American thoroughfares designated as an "All American Road and Scenic Byway."

Older Hotel-Casinos

Sahara, Riviera, Tropicana *(left)*, and Bally's are among the few surviving hotel-casinos of the 1950s to 1970s. Their façades and landscaping are grand but not over-the-top, reflecting the postwar era. Room prices are relatively low.

For more on the Strip **See pp70–77**

Theme Casinos

The MGM Grand, Treasure Island – now called TI *(see p33)*, Monte Carlo, and Luxor *(see p72)* were all built in the early 1990s. As their names suggest, they are designed around themes. MGM Grand features a lion enclosure with real lions, TI *(right)* stages performances in Sirens' Cove. Ancient Egypt is the theme of the Luxor.

Fashion Show Mall

Fashion Show Mall *(see p52)* proudly upholds the Las Vegas maxim that "bigger is better". This upscale mega mall houses 250 luxury shops and restaurants, and no fewer than eight major department stores are anchors here.

The Forum Shops at Caesars

A Las Vegas must-see, the Forum Shops *(see pp26–7, above)* combine entertainment, dining, and shopping. Let your taste buds tingle on a burger while your eyes feast on scenes from ancient Rome.

Hole-in-the-Wall Businesses

Clinging to life between the skyscrapers are simple one-story buildings that house everything from snack shops to tour operators. In one storefront operation men hand-roll cigars.

Hawaiian Marketplace

Located in the center of the Strip between Flamingo and Tropicana, this massive island-themed plaza encloses retail, dining, and entertainment areas.

Impersonators

Elvis lives – at least, his numerous reincarnations do. Elvis Presley and Marilyn Monroe impersonators, among others, are a routine sight on the Strip. They perform in nostalgia shows; some even perform marriage ceremonies. Keep your eyes open, though: some real celebrities live here too!

The Mob

As is vividly portrayed in the 1995 Robert de Niro movie *Casino*, organized crime and Las Vegas were natural bedfellows for several decades from the 1940s. Gangsters were drawn like magpies to the glittering coins piling up effortlessly in so many slot machines. Bugsy Siegel was the trailblazer with his Flamingo Hotel *(see p30)*, while Midwest crime boss Moe Dalitz opened the Desert Inn in 1950. These days, improved regulation and policing appear to have eliminated Mob involvement.

The Five Megaresorts

Bellagio *(see pp14–15)* Venetian *(pp20–21, right)*, Wynn Las Vegas *(pp22–3)*, Mandalay Bay *(p32)*, and Paris *(p33)* have all opened since 1998. Once you are installed there is no need to venture out again: all your desires are catered for.

For more on gambling **See pp122–5**

9

🔟 Hoover Dam

Before the construction of the Hoover Dam early last century, the mighty Colorado River frequently flooded countless acres of farmland in southern California and Mexico. A series of studies into how to tame the rampaging river led in 1928 to the Boulder Canyon Project Act and the subsequent construction of the dam. This colossus of concrete – a triumph of engineering – not only provides flood control and generates electricity, but is also a huge tourist attraction, with nearly a million visitors a year.

The top of the dam

❷ Before you leave Las Vegas, stock up on beverages and mouthwatering sandwiches at Capriotti's Sandwich Shop (322 W. Sahara) to have as a picnic later on a Lake Mead beach.

❻ Take a cruise that does not include meals: it will be cheaper and give you more time to take in the surroundings.

Drive along the west shore of Lake Mead on highways 166 and 167, to access the Valley of Fire and Lost City Museum *(see p98)*.

• Map T2 • 30 miles (50 km) SE of Las Vegas
• Hoover Dam Visitors Center, Hwy 93, Hoover Dam, Boulder City, NV
• 702 494 2517
• Open 9am–5pm daily
• Tour reservations 866 730 9097 (toll free)
• www.usbr.gov/lc/hooverdam

Top 10 Sights

1. Hoover Dam Overlook
2. Hoover Dam Visitors Center
3. Self-guided Tours
4. Lake Mead
5. Black Canyon River Raft Trips
6. Lake Mead Cruises
7. Scuba Diving
8. Boulder City/ Hoover Dam Museum
9. Construction Workers' Houses
10. Commercial District, Boulder City

Hoover Dam Overlook 1

For a lasting first impression, stop at the overlook on Highway 93 as you approach the dam from Las Vegas. The vista point is often crowded, but stop anyway: the sight of 3.2 million cu yards (2.6 million cu m) of concrete, standing 727 ft (221 m) high and erected by thousands of workers laboring around the clock for four years, is truly awe-inspiring.

Hoover Dam Visitors Center 2

Audiovisual and theater presentations as well as multimedia exhibits explain the processes and perils involved in building this eighth wonder of the modern world. An overlook on top of the center provides an eagle-eye view of the dam, Lake Mead, and the Black Canyon.

Self-guided Tours 3

The tours include a descent to the fifth floor, where you can see the dam's huge turbine generators in operation.

The heart of the dam

For more on the Hoover Dam and Lake Mead **See pp92–7**

Lake Mead

The dam's lake is the largest man-made body of water in the USA. Its 700 miles (1,120 km) of shoreline boast forests, canyons, and flower-rich meadows; its waters abound with fish. Boulder Beach offers the best swimming.

Lake Mead Cruises

The lake's shores come to colorful life from the deck of a boat *(left)*. You'll see sandy beaches and rocks of every hue. There's wildlife, too – look out for burros, jack rabbits, lizards, and the occasional bighorn sheep.

Scuba Diving

An unusual underwater scene greets divers: in addition to fish, there is a submerged factory where the dam's concrete was mixed, and the drowned community of St. Thomas. Take a trip with a local company; certified divers can rent scuba gear.

Black Canyon River Raft Trips

The Colorado River flows lazily below the dam, so rafting is pleasant rather than of the white-knuckle variety. The trip takes a little more than three hours to make the 12-mile (19-km) trip to Willow Beach. Look out for petroglyphs carved in the rock, and ringbolts: in the days before the dam these were used to winch steam boats through Ringbolt Rapids.

Boulder City/ Hoover Dam Museum

The dam and the people who built it are the focus of this museum, housed in the historic Boulder Dam Hotel *(see p93, above)*. Don't miss the film chronicling the dam's construction. Memorabilia, photos, and posters give insights into life in the 1930s.

Construction Workers' Houses, Boulder City

Up to 8,000 dam workers were housed here, and although many of the buildings have disappeared, cottages 1–12 look much as they did when they were built.

Commercial District, Boulder City

Walk back into 1930s America. The arcaded, southwestern-style buildings were the precursors of today's shopping plazas. Boulder Dam Hotel, by contrast, is in southern colonial style.

Ancient Peoples

Archeologists disagree about how long humans have lived in the desert along the Colorado River. There were certainly people living downstream from the dam 3–4,000 years ago, and possibly as many as 8,000. The Patayans were among the first Native Americans known to live in the broader tri-state area (Nevada, Arizona, California), appearing in about 900 AD; they lived in brush shelters and ate pulverized seeds and plants. Their descendants split into the Hualapai and Mojave tribes.

Glitter Gulch

During the 1980s and early 1990s, as the Strip became ever more glamorous, the downtown area – including the stretch along Fremont Street known as Glitter Gulch – went further and further into decline. City fathers and casino owners alike agreed that something had to be done to reverse the process and took action to see that it was. The resulting efforts have revitalized the area. Development is ongoing, with the opening of new restaurants and cocktail bars offering a greater range of entertainment for visitors.

Fremont Street

🍴 For a memorable meal, try Florida Café Restaurante Cubano (1401 Las Vegas Boulevard S.).

⚠️ Don't wander away from the bright lights after dark. High-crime areas still exist not far from Glitter Gulch *(see p131).*

Arrive a few minutes before the hour to see the light and sound show at the Fremont Street Experience. Then explore the shops and casinos or enjoy the stage entertainment until the next show begins.

• Map J–K4 • Golden Gate, 1 Fremont St, 702 385 1906
• Golden Nugget, 129 E. Fremont St, 702 385 7111
• Binion's, 128 Fremont St, 702 382 1600 or 800 237 6537
• Lady Luck 206 N. 3rd St, 702 477 3000 or 800 523 9582

Top 10 Sights

1. Glitter Gulch Lights
2. Fremont Street Experience
3. Signs of the Past
4. Las Vegas's First Casino
5. Fremont Street Pedestrian Promenade
6. Golden Nugget
7. Binion's
8. Triple George Grill
9. Casino Characters
10. Entertainment

Glitter Gulch Lights

The heart of downtown has earned its name for reasons that become obvious as soon as you set foot here. This is one of the brightest places on earth – so much so that you can stand on the street at midnight and read a newspaper. Even before the Fremont Street Experience was conceived, the country's leading neon designers and lighting engineers were strutting their stuff here.

Fremont Street Experience

A major part of the downtown revival was the transformation in 1995 of one four-block stretch of Fremont Street into a pedestrian mall, covered with a 90-ft (27-m) high "Space Frame" containing more than 12.5 million lights. Every night, from 8pm until midnight, an hourly sound and light extravaganza entertains the crowds below. (See also pp78–9.)

Fremont Street Experience

Signs of the Past

Las Vegas Vic *(see p80)* has been waving to passersby on Fremont Street since 1951. More illuminating insights into the history of neon are at the Neon Museum *(see p45)* on the corner of Fremont and Las Vegas Blvd.

Las Vegas's First Casino

The place where it all started is the Sal Sagev Hotel on Fremont Street, which is now the Golden Gate. The strange-looking original name makes sense in mirror-writing. The new place is famous not so much for gambling as for its shrimp cocktails.

Triple George Grill

This popular restaurant is reminiscent of a 1950s San Francisco diner, with its black and white tile floor and wooden booths. Located at 201 N. 3rd Street, the restaurant often hosts the best piano players in town.

Golden Nugget

The four-star Golden Nugget is the best-value hotel in the city (rates can fall as low as $60 in the off-season). Its casino is also first-rate *(see p37)*. Try the Carson Street Café for its relaxing ambience – and also for some great people-watching.

Binion's

Dallas bootlegger and gambler Benny Binion established the property in 1951, and it was owned until recently by his descendants. The biggest names in poker continue to play at Binion's, although the World Series of Poker has moved to Rio *(see p36.)* The hotel-casino is worth a visit to appreciate its old-time atmosphere.

Casino Characters

If you ever want to get from one end of Fremont Street to the other, you will have to resist the charms of an assortment of exotically dressed showgirls, mermaids, and cowboys hired by the casinos to entice people in.

Entertainment

In addition to the production shows and lounge acts at most of the hotels *(see pp42–3)*, entertainment centers on Fremont Street. It's a popular venue for parades and perform-ances by musical groups. *(See also p82.)*

Glitter Gulch Beginnings

For 20 years after its incorporation, entertain-ment in Las Vegas was limited to a few bars and brothels in the red-light district downtown. The legalization of gambling and arrival of 5,000 dam-construction workers in 1931 changed all that. Casinos opened on Fremont Street, and tourists began to arrive. World War II personnel and their families gave Las Vegas another population surge in the 1940s, and casino building continued apace after the war – as it does to this day.

Fremont Street Pedestrian Promenade

Another mid-1990s downtown improvement is the walkway between Main and 4th Streets, which is decked with flowers, colorful street vendors' carts, and strolling performers.

For the top hotels and casinos in Las Vegas **See pp32–7**

🔟 Bellagio

From the flower arrangements in the halls to the fixtures in the bathtubs, Bellagio, built in 1998, is the epitome of perfection. The goal of Steve Wynn, who originally conceived this grand monument to leisure, was to create a hotel "that would exemplify absolute quality while emphasizing romance and elegance – romance in the literary sense, a place of ideal beauty and comfort; the world everyone hopes for, as it might be if everything were just right." Most people agree that Wynn achieved his goal.

Façade of the Bellagio

🍽 For a leisurely lunch in a tranquil setting, reserve a table on the terrace at Olives, overlooking Lake Bellagio.

🌀 For a real treat, indulge yourself with an afternoon spent at the hotel's luxurious spa. Group booking can be arranged for brides and bridesmaids, and there's even a treatment menu specifically for men.

To enjoy the full effect of Bellagio's fountain show, cross the street and go to the observation level of the Eiffel Tower at Paris Las Vegas.

• Map Q1–2 • 3600 Las Vegas Blvd S. • Reservations 888 987 6667
• General info 702 693 7111 • www.bellagio.com • $$$$$ (for price categories see p89)

Top 10 Features

1. Italianate Theme
2. Lobby Ceiling
3. Via Bellagio
4. Conservatory and Botanical Gardens
5. Casino
6. Gallery of Fine Art
7. Theater
8. Restaurants
9. Courtyard
10. Meeting and Business Facilities

Italianate Theme

Fronting on a pristine 8.5-acre lake with a tree-lined boulevard beyond, this extraordinary resort hotel was built to resemble an idyllic village on the shores of Italy's Lake Como. The Italianate theme is carried through the entire property – its original 3,000-room tower, the Spa Tower, 19 dining options, and two wedding chapels – creating an atmosphere of opulence. Building this representation of Italy cost $1.975 billion.

Lobby Ceiling

Visitors are greeted by a dazzling 2,000 sq ft (186 sq m) garden of glass flowers – the Fiore di Como – suspended from the lobby ceiling. The creator was Dale Chihuly, the first American artist to be designated a national treasure; amazingly, every single flower is different.

For more theme hotels See pp32–3

Via Bellagio
You are only likely to frequent Bellagio's shopping promenade if you have deep pockets. The establishments are as elegant as the Via itself, numbering among them such names as Prada, Tiffany & Co., Chanel, Giorgio Armani, Dior, Hermes, Gucci, and Yves St Laurent. *(See also p52.)*

Casino
Aesthetically this is the most pleasing casino in Las Vegas, less flamboyant and more sophisticated than the rest. Slot-machine carousels are fringed with specially designed fabrics rather than the ubiquitous neon tubing, and custom-made carpets provide a stylish relief from the norm.

Gallery of Fine Art
Bellagio's art gallery hosts major temporary exhibitions of important international artists past and present in conjunction with other large art galleries and museums in North America and around the world.

Theater
Designed for Cirque du Soleil's spectacular production "O" *(see p38)*, the theater combines Old World magnificence (it is styled after the Paris Opera) with cutting-edge technology. Central to the production is a 1.5 million gallon (6.8 million liter) pool, which can be remodeled to meet each act's needs.

Restaurants
Bellagio's superb restaurants include Le Cirque, Michael Mina, Noodles, Jasmine, and Yellowtail. Picasso *(see p46)* holds the coveted Mobil five stars and is decorated with originals.

Conservatory and Botanical Gardens
Keen gardeners and plant-lovers who stay here regularly will be rewarded with floral displays that change with each season and Chinese New Year. Each change employs the services of no fewer than 150 professionals.

Courtyard
With its Italianate columns and statuary, five outdoor pools, and four spas *(see p65)*, the formal courtyard at Bellagio is glorious for morning and evening strolls. During the middle part of the day, it is transformed into a scene of poolside cabanas, chaises (sunbeds), and umbrella tables, with bronzed sun-worshipers sipping cool drinks.

Meeting and Business Facilities
Bellagio has the capacity to host conference groups of up to 5,500 people in 50 different rooms, including three ballrooms. A professional staff is on hand to assist with needs such as word processing.

High Rollers
High rollers – gambling's big spenders – are courted by every major casino. Who qualifies (based on the amount he or she bets) varies a good deal, but a really big spender – someone who wagers thousands in an evening – will get superstar treatment from the top hotels. They may get flown to Las Vegas in a private jet, put up in a luxurious suite, and given carte blanche to order whatever they want from the hotel. Like superstars, high rollers are also treated with the ultimate discretion, so you may not spot one.

For advice on booking accommodations See p135

Grand Canyon

"Overwhelming" and "humbling" are the words most often used to describe the Grand Canyon experience. One of the world's most awesome sights, the canyon is 277 miles (443 km) long, 10 miles (16 km) wide, and as deep as a mile (1.6 km) in places. Because of the vast differences in elevation between floor and rim, the canyon encompasses a range of desert and mountain habitats. The South Rim, easier to access via road than the North Rim, is a five-hour drive away from Las Vegas.

Layers of the canyon wall

See p106 for great places to eat at the Grand Canyon.

The South Rim of the Grand Canyon is accessible by road year-round, but the North Rim road and facilities are closed from November to mid-May.

You will need a permit to camp outside the official campsites within the national park. Apply in advance at the Backcountry Information Center.

- Map V2 • South Rim 271 miles (434 km), North Rim 255 miles (408 km) E of Las Vegas
- South Rim Visitor Center, Canyon View Information Plaza, Mather Point, open 8am–5pm daily, 928 638 7888
- www.nps.gov/grca
- Admission charge to enter national park $20 per vehicle or $10 per pedestrian

Top 10 Features

1. Flyovers
2. Flatwater Adventure
3. Visitor Centers
4. Hiking Trails
5. Overlooks
6. Whitewater Rafting
7. Skywalk
8. Tusayan Village
9. California Condors
10. Golden Aspen

1 Flyovers
Airplane flights to the Grand Canyon rank among the most popular day trips from Las Vegas (see p109).

2 Flatwater Adventure
If you want a taste of canyon rafting, sign up for a one-day flatwater rafting tour. The tours begin at the Glen Canyon Dam and travel 15 miles (24 km) downstream to Lee's Ferry, which is the entrance to Marble Canyon (see p105) and the beginning of the Grand Canyon itself. Along the way, near-vertical canyon walls rise high above the lake-like surface of the river.

3 Visitor Centers
Information centers at the North and South Rims of the canyon supply free maps as well as *The Guide*, which has general park information, *The Jr. Ranger Guide*, listing children's activities, and *The Accessibility Guide*, with information for disabled visitors. The Grand Canyon Railway *(below)* runs from the town of Williams to Grand Canyon Village, close to the South Rim Visitor Center. Great observation points are near both centers.

For more on the canyon and places to stay See pp98–109

Hiking Trails

Ranking high with South Rim hikers are the South Kaibab, Bright Angel, and Rim trails *(see p108)*. Popular North Rim day hikes include those along the North Kaibab, Bright Angel Point, and Widforss trails. Don't attempt to hike to the canyon floor and back in one day: get an overnight permit.

Overlooks

For the grandest of grand views, head for the Yaki, Grandview, and Moran Points on the South and East Rims. You can see almost to Utah from the top of the 70-ft (23-m) Watchtower. Yavapai Observation Station and Maricopa Point, at the park's east entrance (Desertview), have marvelous vistas. Motorists can use the Desert View Drive (Hwy 64) along the South Rim, following the edge for 26 miles (42 km). Hermits Road hugs the North Rim for 8 miles (13 km), but is closed from October to May due to heavy snowfall.

California Condors

Standing over 3 ft (1 m) tall and with a wingspan of about 9 ft (3 m), the rare California condor may be spotted flying over the South Canyon Rim in summer.

Golden Aspen

In the fall, the North Rim explodes in a brilliant yellow blaze, as thick stands of aspen trees turn a golden hue.

Whitewater Rafting

Dozens of companies, like Canyon Explorations *(see p109)*, offer whitewater rafting trips along the Colorado on the canyon floor. Trips vary in length from 6 to 16 days.

Skywalk

Thrill-seeking nature lovers must visit the Grand Canyon Skywalk on the South Rim. The glass platform allows you to look straight down to the Colorado River 4,000 ft (1,200 m) below.

Tusayan Village

Ruins of rock dwellings inhabited by ancestors of the Hopi Indians around AD 1200 are preserved between South Rim Village and the park's east entrance. On display at Tusayan Ruins and Museum are artifacts, recreated dwellings, and exhibits of contemporary local tribes. *Grand Canyon – The Hidden Secrets* is shown on a giant IMAX screen in Tusayan village.

Exploration of the Canyon

In 1869, Major John Wesley Powell, a veteran of the American Civil War, led an exploration party along the Colorado River through the canyon. On August 28, three of the men left the group at the rim of Separation Canyon. They were killed by Native Americans. Ironically, it was the following day that Powell's expedition emerged safely from the gorge, completing the first exploration ever made of the Grand Canyon.

Following pages **The South Rim at dusk, Grand Canyon**

🏆10 The Venetian

Some months after the opening of Bellagio (see pp14–15), Sheldon Adelson was ready to unveil the Venetian. Everyone held their breath. Could anyone possibly replicate Venice? Of course not: Adelson imitated this most romantic of Italian cities just enough to catch the flavor but without sacrificing Las Vegas pizzazz. Since opening, the Venetian has announced a number of added attractions – a theater for live performances, a nightclub (see p42), plus extra eateries. Venice? Not really. But exciting – definitely!

Arcade in the grounds of the Venetian

🍽 Splurge on a meal at Wolfgang Puck's Postrio, named by Hotels *Magazine* as "one of the ten greatest restaurants in the world."

🎭 It is almost as much fun – and a lot less expensive – to watch the gondoliers from land as it is to actually ride in the gondolas.

If possible, visit the Venetian when there is a full moon and the crowds have thinned: by moonlight it is breathtaking.

- Map P2 • 3355 Las Vegas Blvd S.
- 702 414 1000 or 888 283 6423
- www.venetian.com
- $$$$$ suites only (for price categories see p89)

Top 10 Features

1. Architecture and Ambience
2. Lobby
3. Grand Canal
4. St. Mark's Square
5. Canal Shoppes
6. Restaurants
7. Madame Tussaud's
8. Special Events
9. Palazzo Las Vegas
10. Casino

1 Architecture and Ambience

The grandeur of Venice meets Las Vegas glitz, and the results are surprisingly spectacular. True, the Grand Canal is only 1,200 ft (350 m) long as opposed to 2.5 miles (4 km), but any lack of authenticity is more than made up for by the festive Las Vegas ambience.

2 Lobby

Reproductions of frescoes framed in 24-karat gold adorn the domed and vaulted ceilings. Marble floors, classical columns, costumed courtiers, and a giant overview of the real Venice all serve to transport the imagination.

3 Grand Canal

Push the boat out and hire the Venetian's very own Wedding Gondola for your marriage ceremony! You can even sail under the Rialto Bridge.

For more theme hotels See pp32–3

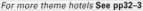

Canal Shoppes

5 The galaxy of goodies in the shops along the canal *(see p53; left)* satisfy a wide range of tastes: there are magic tricks at Houdini's and ice-cream cones at Haagen Däzs; there are pearls at Mikimoto and smart sportswear at Banana Republic. Travel by gondola or meander the (rather long) walkway linking the stores.

Restaurants

6 Stars of the Venetian's gastronomic line-up include Wolfgang Puck's Postrio (Asian-Mediterranean cuisine), Emeril Lagasse's Delmonico Steakhouse, TAO Asian Bistro and Nightclub *(see p42)*, and Joachim Splichal's Pinot Brasserie (French-California fare).

Palazzo Las Vegas

9 This 2008 addition to the Venetian is a stunning, all-suite hotel-casino. There are shops, restaurants, and great entertainment, including shows and a nightclub.

Casino

10 Set in the Doge's Palace, the vast casino has 110 table games and 2,000 slot machines. On the walls of the high rollers' "Renaissance Room" hang works by Tiepolo, Tintoretto, and Titian. Costumed singers belt out arias in counterpoint to the cacophony of slot-machine bells and clanging coins.

Madame Tussaud's

7 In a building fashioned after the library on St. Mark's Square, the wax museum *(above)* opened in 1999 and soon became a top attraction; some visitors say the figures are even more lifelike than those in the London original *(see pp28–9)*.

St. Mark's Square

4 So the geography isn't exactly as per the original, but even if you notice you probably won't care – the total effect is, aesthetically, extremely pleasing, perhaps more so than at any of the other new resorts.

Special Events

8 Throughout the year, the Venetian hosts events, such as a Special Celebrity Invitational Dinner Gala on Super Bowl weekend, and dragon dances during Chinese New Year.

High Hurdles

The journey of a major hotel-casino from the drawing board to the grand opening is a long and often tortuous process. Of course, plans must be submitted and approved by city government and county commissioners. But the most rigorous scrutiny is reserved not for the building but for those involved in owning and managing the casino. These people are vetted by the Nevada Gaming Commission and subjected to a thorough background check before a gaming license is issued.

For more on museums See pp44–5

Wynn Las Vegas

Wynn Las Vegas is a show-stopper. Built on the site of the legendary Desert Inn – once owned by Howard Hughes – the Strip's newest mega-resort was designed to captivate the highest of high-rollers and the biggest of the big spenders. Over-the-top opulence, from its extravagant villas to the auto-mobiles in the Ferrari-Maserati showroom, reigns supreme. The new Encore Suites at Wynn tower brings even more luxury to this world-class resort. Its grounds are spectacular, too, with an artificial mountain and small lake.

Poolside cabana

○ Of all the eateries at Wynn Las Vegas, The Buffet features everything from sushi to steak, and an all-you-can-eat buffet. Breakfast: $17.95; lunch: $21.95; dinner: $33.95 (Sun–Thu) and $37.95 (Fri–Sat); weekend brunch: $34.95 (with champagne; $24.95 without).

● Wear walking shoes if you want to explore the resort as there is a lot of ground to cover.

Less expensive food is available in several restaurants across the street at Fashion Show Mall.

• Map Q2
• 3131 Las Vegas Blvd S.
• 702 770 7100, 1 800 320 9966 (toll free)
• www.wynnlasvegas. com
• $$$$$ (for price categories see p89)

Top 10 Features

1 Casino
2 Le Rêve
3 Suites
4 Fine Dining
5 Golf Course
6 Tryst
7 The Esplanade
8 Wedding Salons
9 The Gardens
10 The Spa

Casino
The 111,000 sq-ft (10,200 sq-m) casino seems more intimate than its size would indicate. The gambling stakes on the slot machines and table games are higher than at other casinos, reflecting the upmarket clientele. The décor is lavish: natural tone draperies fringed in fiesta colors mute the noise, and there's not a flashing light or neon sign in sight. The tile walkway provides natural light and views over the indoor oases.

Le Rêve
This aquatic masterpiece is the work of Franco Dragone, who also created shows for Cirque du Soleil. The abstract production features fabulous costumes, jaw-dropping gymnastics, elegant synchronised swimming, and comedy. Shows take place in a theater in the round, where the stage is surrounded by a pool, so there are no restricted views. Be warned: seats in rows A to C always get wet.

For more theme hotels **See pp32–3**

Suites
3 The wall-to-wall floor-to-ceiling windows of the 300-plus suites look out on the Strip, golf course, or mountains. All guest quarters are enormous and feature European linen, elegant furniture, DVD players, and flat-screen TVs in both living and bath areas.

Fine Dining
4 Wynn's restaurants have celebrity chefs preparing some of the city's tastiest dishes. Okada is renowned for upscale Japanese cuisine with the likes of Kobe carpaccio, and *foie gras* with barbecued eel. Alex, the resort's elegant signature restaurant, focuses on French favorites.

Golf Course
5 Owner Steve Wynn and golfer Tom Fazio collaborated in re-designing this huge course by moving more than 800,000 cu ft (23,000 cu m) of desert sand, repositioning trees, and adding features including the high waterfall that players walk under to get from the 18th hole to the traditional-style clubhouse.

Tryst
6 One of the most sophisticated and impressive clubs in the city, Tryst contains a marble staircase and the requisite pole dancing stage. The club is decorated with red velvet walls, and features a 94-ft (28-m) waterfall, and a patio that wraps around a semicircular lagoon. Table service costs $450 for three people, but drinks can also be bought at the bar.

The Esplanade
7 Behind the brass, glass, and chrome façades of Cartier, Oscar de la Renta, Judith Leiber, Manolo Blahnik, and almost two dozen other high-end stores lies temptation galore for visiting billionaires and gamblers. Window shoppers can admire the cars at the Ferrari-Maserati dealership nearby.

Wedding Salons
8 For visitors planning to marry here, there are two wedding chapels with private foyers and bridal rooms. The Lilac Salon seats 65 guests, while the Lavender Salon accommodates 120. The Primrose Court provides a romantic setting for outdoor weddings under a canopy of trees.

The Gardens
9 Wynn's beautiful gardens bloom whatever the season. Mature trees, dazzling beds, and manicured bushes line exterior walkways. Inside, atriums and mini-oases decorate public areas.

The Spa
10 Hotel guests can indulge in a range of wraps, massages, and other treatments. Clients can enjoy them in one of the 45 tranquil treatment rooms *(below)*, or at the poolside cabana *(top left)*.

Steve Wynn
If any one man can be credited with shaping the Las Vegas Strip, it is Steve Wynn. The creative casino magnate opened the Mirage in 1989 and a new era began – one that impacted on gaming around the world. When Wynn unveiled the Bellagio nine years later, the gauntlet for hotel-casino excellence was thrown down and the mega-resort trend was born. He describes his latest creation, Wynn Las Vegas, as "the most expensive, the most complex, the most ambitious structure ever built in the world … "

For more on shopping **See pp52–3**

Red Rock Canyon

About 225 million years ago, everything at Red Rock Canyon was covered by an inland sea. The escarpment, formations, and caves were created after that sea evaporated and wind and rain began sculpting the land. This remarkable desert region lies just 10 miles (16 km) west of Las Vegas. A conservation area since 1990, it is protected from the encroaching asphalt and grass of city expansion. The 13-mile (21-km) scenic road that loops off Hwy 159 provides a good overview, but the best way to explore this part of the Mojave Desert is on foot.

Desert lizard

🥯 Stop at one of the Einstein Bagels shops in Las Vegas for a picnic lunch to eat at the Willow Spring picnic area.

♿ Trails that are suitable for wheelchairs start from the Visitor Center, at Willow Spring, and the Overlook.

You will need a permit if you want to camp overnight or go rock-climbing at Red Rock Canyon. Apply at the Visitor Center.

Take the usual precautions when visiting a desert area *(see p133).*

• Map T2 • 20 miles (35 km) W of Las Vegas
• Visitor Center, 1000 Scenic Drive, open 7am–5pm daily • 702 515 5350
• www.redrockcanyon. blm.gov • Admission charge $5 per vehicle
• Campground $10 per night, per site

Top 10 Features

1. Red Rock Vista
2. Visitor Center
3. Hikes and Guided Walks
4. Desert Tortoises
5. Children's Discovery Trail
6. Petroglyphs and Pictographs
7. Thirteen-Mile Drive
8. Bookstore
9. Desert Whiptail Lizards
10. Tinajas

Red Rock Vista
The view from this overlook (about one mile past the Hwy 159 turnoff to the Canyon) is of the Red Rock escarpment itself, which rises a breathtaking 3,000 ft (1,000 m) from the valley floor. Time your trip to get here at either sunrise or sunset when the colors of this Aztec sandstone are at their sensational best.

Visitor Center
The Visitor Center *(below)* has area Maps and staff on hand to answer questions. You can peer through telescopes on the viewing terrace at the detail of surrounding formations. A small museum contains geological and natural history displays.

Elephant Rock, Calico Hills

Hikes and Guided Walks
Of more than 30 miles (50 km) of hiking trails within the canyon, the most popular include those to Ice Box Canyon (it really is cooler there) and Oak Creek. Guided walks focus on aspects of the environment such as native wildflowers and the area's geology.

For more parks and preserves near Las Vegas **See pp98–109**

4 Desert Tortoises
Look out for brown-shelled tortoises, which, with their lifespan of up to 100 years, may outlive you. They dig burrows in the desert and spend at least 95 percent of their long lives below ground. Astonishingly, adult tortoises can survive for a year without water.

6 Petroglyphs and Pictographs
The area around Willow Springs contains some fascinating prehistoric rock carvings and paintings. The exact meaning of many of the incised and painted symbols is not known, but because the area's early inhabitants were hunters and gatherers, it is believed that many symbolize the procuring of food.

9 Desert Whiptail Lizards
Common to the western United States, these small lizards have pointed snouts and forked tongues, which help them eat termites, spiders, scorpions, centipedes, and other lizards. Recognize them by the four or five light stripes along the back, and yellow- or cream-colored belly with scattered dark spots.

10 Tinajas
Prevalent in the Calico Hills and at White Rock Spring, tinajas (or tanks) are naturally formed rock catchments for water. They serve as drinking basins for wildlife and so are good places to head for photo opportunities.

5 Children's Discovery Trail
Ask at the visitor center about their especially strong program for children, which includes educational funbooks and incentives for learning. Up near Willow Creek is the Children's Discovery Trail to Lost Creek. Less than a mile long, this fun round-trip highlights points of interest along the way. Pick up the free accompanying workbook at the Vistor Center.

7 Thirteen-Mile Drive
The main scenic loop (above) is a one-way road taking in the Rainbow and Bridge mountains, and the Calico Hills. Designated stopping points for views are scattered along the way. Head for Willow Spring or Red Spring for picnic areas. Most of the hiking trails are accessible from car parks on the loop.

8 Bookstore
The Visitor Center bookstore covers the local flora, fauna, and geology. Excellent Southwest-themed books for children include *Gullywasher* by Joyce Rossi and *Cowboy Country* by Ann Herbert Scott.

Mountain Biking
Designated mountain bike trails include the 41-mile (65-km) Red Rock-Wilson Cliff Loop, with a mile-long extension to the north peak vista at the top of Wilson Cliffs. The full ride takes five to eight hours to complete and is classed as very difficult, but the views of the Sandstone Bluffs and Red Rock Canyon lands are magnificent. Other rides include those totally within Red Rock, the Bristlecone Pine trail in the Spring Mountain Recreation Area, and one through Blue Diamond back to Las Vegas.

The Forum Shops at Caesars

"So many shops and so little time" is the complaint of most first-time visitors to the Forum Shops. Opals from Australia, an endangered species store, couturier clothes, and art galleries – there are 160 stores in all. The common areas of the complex are open 24 hours a day, so the savvy travelers who want to window shop and get close-up looks at the Forum's fountains and buildings will stroll its lanes in the wee hours of the morning.

Cheesecake Factory

🔵 Have lunch at one of the restaurants with a sidewalk café, from where you can watch the passing parades.

🟢 Pick up a map of the shops at the Las Vegas Convention & Visitors Authority *(see p115).*

Walking from the parking garage to the shops is a shorter trek than through the enormous casino.

If you're visiting with youngsters, set aside some time to visit the child-pleasing FAO Schwarz toy store.

• Map P1–2 • Caesars Palace Hotel, 3570 Las Vegas Blvd S.
• 702 893 4800
• Shops open 10am–11pm Mon–Thu, 10am–midnight Fri–Sun
• Dining reservations 702 731 7731
• www.caesars.com

Top 10 Shops and Sights

1. Festival Fountain
2. Lost City of Atlantis
3. Sky Ceiling
4. Chinois Restaurant
5. Upscale Fashion Shops
6. FAO Schwarz
7. Planet Hollywood
8. Wolfgang Puck's Spago
9. 3-D Motion Simulator
10. Cheescake Factory

Festival Fountain
Focal point of the original group of Forum Shops, the Festival Fountain is guarded by four animatronic statues of Roman notables, who on the hour from 11am talk about the days of the Roman Empire. The production generated excitement when the center opened in 1992.

Lost City of Atlantis
Created in 1997, this attraction *(below)* is the centerpiece for a newer section of the Forum Shops. Atop the giant circular monument is a statue of Poseidon. Rare species of Atlantic Ocean fish swim in a 50,000-gallon aquarium, the focus of a feature presentation held every half hour from 11:30am.

The Sky above the Forum

Sky Ceiling
The domed ceiling of the Forum Shops simulates a constantly changing sky. The morning sun shines; afternoon clouds float by; evening stars twinkle.

Chinois Restaurant
Wolfgang Puck's Chinois offers an eclectic blend of Asian and French cuisine. Charcoal-grilled Szechuan beef, wok-fried lobster, and sizzling whole catfish are all prepared with a French twist. *(See also p47.)*

For more on shopping See pp52–5 & 116

5 Upscale Fashion Shops

The shopping mall is bigger than ever after a 2008 expansion. Top designer brands including Fendi, Gucci and Valentino, help this mall retain its self-proclaimed title as the "shopping wonder of the world".

7 Planet Hollywood

This enormous restaurant is crammed with Hollywood memorabilia. Framed movie posters, celebrity photographs, costumes worn in famous films, and movie props make this café – according to its advertisements – one of the largest repositories for movie mementos in the world. California-style cuisine features out-of-the-ordinary sandwiches and salads.

8 Wolfgang Puck's Spago

Spago was the first of the celebrity chef restaurants on the Vegas scene, starting the trend that is upstaging the city's traditionally famous buffets *(see pp48–9)* with upscale dining. Duck with roasted garlic polenta and other unusual combinations are among the rotating specials at this sophisticated dining spot.

6 FAO Schwarz

Walk through a huge Trojan horse to enter this toy store. Inside, the sheer volume of toys is overwhelming. Character dolls range from storybook favorites Eloise and Madeline to G.I. Joe and Harry Potter. Computer toys include Virtual FAO Baby and Virtual Playroom. A robotic puppy named Techno walks, talks, begs, sniffs, snores, and plays with his ball. Buttercup Hippo, the Big Piano Dance Mat, and the Tommy Hilfiger Dolls are sold only by FAO Schwarz.

9 3-D Motion Simulator

Don special 3-D glasses to experience the amazing full effects of four rides here. One features a spaceship ride through the galaxy, another simulates a submarine race to the South Pole. The roller coaster thrill ride is not for people who suffer car sickness, and the timid should avoid the haunted graveyard ride. Tickets can be purchased individually or as a package.

10 Cheesecake Factory

With more than 200 items on the menu, Cheesecake Factory has everything from hot spinach and cheese dip with tortilla chips, bruschetta, and Tex Mex eggrolls to Triple Chocolate Brownie Truffle Cheesecake. Entrées include a teriyaki chicken that incorporates banana slices, pineapple, and brown sugar.

Commerce or Entertainment?

In most US cities, shopping is an end in itself: go to the mall, make purchases, return home. In Las Vegas, however, shopping has the added dimension of being coupled with entertainment. The Forum Shops and some of the new hotels, including Paris and the Venetian, all have musicians, singers, mimes, and other performers strolling along the shopping arcades entertaining the crowds. It's all free and it adds to the glamour and excitement *(see also pp52–3)*.

For more on Caesars Palace Hotel **See p32**

Madame Tussaud's Wax Museum

Everything about Las Vegas is larger than life. At Madame Tussaud's (within the Venetian Hotel) this is literally true – and the precise figure is 2 percent larger. Each waxwork figure in the museum is made marginally bigger than its real-life counterpart, because wax shrinks as it ages. For authenticity, many items of clothing and props were purchased at celebrity auctions. Rings on the figures' fingers are regularly cleaned; hair must be washed and makeup retouched. And, as with real people, the figures' clothes frequently need cleaning.

Madame Tussaud's
entrance

For a quick lunch on the way there or back, try the Venetian's Food Court.

To avoid big crowds, arrive soon after the museum opens and visit the rooms in reverse order.

Save time for browsing around the gift shop: the merchandise is more imaginative than you might expect.

• Map P2 • St Mark's Library Building within the Venetian Hotel, 3377 Las Vegas Boulevard S
• www.mtvegas.com
• Open 10am–7pm Sun–Thu, 10am–10pm Fri–Sat
• 702 862 7800
• Admission charge $24 for adults, $18 for seniors, $14 for children 7–12

Top 10 Features

1. Frank Sinatra
2. Show-time Legends
3. The Big Night
4. Sports Celebrities
5. Rock and Pop
6. Behind the Scenes Glimpse
7. Finale
8. Souvenir Photos
9. The Building
10. The Gift Shop

Frank Sinatra

Before entering the "Show-time Legends" section of the museum, get acquainted with a young, slender Sinatra *(right)* performing on the stage of the old Sands Hotel. Recordings of Sinatra standards and other stage props enhance the 1950s mood.

Show-time Legends

Come face to face with your idols in a real spine-tingler of a room: eavesdrop on Louis Armstrong chatting with Ella Fitzgerald, and gaze without fear of reproach at Marilyn Monroe, tantalizingly real in a sequined dress.

Frank Sinatra

The Big Night

A Hollywood gala is the setting, and the guest list is impressive. Mingle with the likes of Arnold Schwarzenegger (positively huge at just 2 percent larger than life), Shirley MacLaine, Whoopie Goldberg, Paul Newman, Princess Diana, and Elizabeth Taylor *(left)*; and yes, the hair *is* real.

For more museums See pp44–5

Sports Celebrities

They would never normally be gathered together in the same room, but at Madame Tussaud's you suspend disbelief. Rubbing well-muscled shoulders are stars of track and field, tennis court, and boxing ring. Even with the waxwork enlargement, Russian gymnast Olga Korbut still looks tiny.

The Building

Extending the copycat theme, and in typically grand Las Vegas style, the building itself is a small-scale replica of the library building on the Piazza San Marco in Venice.

The Gift Shop

The gift shop is almost as entertaining as the museum itself. You can choose a wig or a hat that makes you look like your favorite star (well, quite like) – great for kids or for costume parties.

On a more serious note, there's a chocoholics' area, with chocolate body-frosting and other "choco-therapy" items.

Behind the Scenes Glimpse

It can seem a little creepy, but the painstaking process of making the waxwork models *(above)* is fascinating – from taking precise measurements of each celebrity to matching skin tones, dental impressions, eye, and hair color.

Madame Tussaud

Born Anne Marie Grosholtz in Strasbourg, France, in 1761, the future Madame Tussaud inherited a collection of wax figures from her mother's employer when the latter died in 1794. Anne Marie married civil engineer François Tussaud and went to Britain, where she toured her collection for 33 years, finally setting up the exhibit in London. The original collection was destroyed by fire but has been revived in the form of the present London museum and several other versions around the world.

Finale

The somewhat anticlimactic finale is a state-of-the-art, multimedia, theatrical tribute to Las Vegas, featuring music, movie clips, and a special appearance by Elvis.

Souvenir Photos

A must-have souvenir is a photograph of yourself alongside your famous (or infamous) idol. It's a great talking point with your more gullible friends back home.

Rock and Pop

Remember those teenage heartthrobs of yours – Stevie Wonder, Michael Jackson, and Bruce Springsteen? Here you can get closer than you ever imagined. Videos and wrap-around sound help bring the experience to glorious life.

For more about the Venetian Hotel **See pp20–21**

Left **Mormon fort** Center **The Rat Pack** Right **MGM Grand**

🔟 Great Moments in Las Vegas History

1 1855: Mormons Establish a Trading Post

Inhabited for centuries by Native Americans, and encountered by Spanish explorers in 1829, the Las Vegas area was only permanently settled in 1855 when a group of Mormons, led by Brigham Young, established a trading post here.

2 1931: Gambling Legalized in Nevada

The relaxed gaming laws passed in the Silver State in 1931 encouraged widespread participation *(above)*. In reality, betting and gambling were already widespread and, in some forms, legal.

3 1935: Boulder Dam Dedicated by Roosevelt

The greatest hydroelectric project of the 20th century, the Boulder (later Hoover) Dam was begun in 1931 and completed four years later, at a human cost of 96 lives. *(See pp10–11.)*

4 1940s: Air Conditioning and Irrigation Arrive

The ability to keep buildings cool and the greening brought about by irrigation made the Nevada desert far more attractive to developers. In 1941 Los Angeles hotelier Tom Hull bought land three miles south of downtown for $150 an acre and built the 100-room El Rancho motel – a new concept in accommodation.

5 Christmas Day, 1946: Bugsy Siegel Opens the Flamingo Hotel

A handful of hotels and motels followed El Rancho, but only when mobster Benjamin "Bugsy" Siegel built the Flamingo Hotel was the hitherto Wild West feel of the town replaced with the Miami Beach style that was to become the hallmark of the Strip.

6 1960: The Rat Pack Comes to Town

The extravagant Flamingo was widely imitated in the 1950s, and entertainment was an important part of the new casinos' allure. Frank Sinatra performed at the Sands hotel in 1960, with friends including John F. Kennedy in the audience. From then on Vegas became a playground of the so-called Rat Pack (Sinatra, Sammy Davis, Jr., Dean Martin, Peter Lawford, Joey Bishop, *et al*).

7 1966: Howard Hughes Arrives

Hughes's Summa Corporation was a dominant player in the Nevada hotel/casino industry. Legend (which makes up much Las Vegas history) has it that the eccentric billionaire arrived in

For the top hotels **See pp32–3**

town one day by limousine and was whisked up to his suite at the Desert Inn, where he lived as

a recluse for several years, with uncut fingernails and hair.

8 1990s: The Era of the Theme Hotels Begins

In the 1970s and 1980s the hotels became larger and more flamboyant. In 1991 the groundbreaking MGM Grand, Treasure Island, and pyramid-shaped Luxor launched the theme hotel in earnest.

9 1998: Bellagio Opens

Hotelier Steve Wynn set a new standard for Las Vegas hotels with the luxurious Bellagio *(see pp14–15)*. The former owner of the Mirage hotel group (sold to MGM in 2000) is acknowledged as the creative force behind the modern resort concept.

10 2009 Onwards: The New Generation of Resorts

Las Vegas is a dynamic, ever-evolving city. The near future will see the realization of mega resort "cities". Developments including CityCenter, Echelon and Viva offer greater accommodation choice as well as countless restaurants, shops, and entertainment venues.

Bellagio

Famous Residents

1 Jerry Lewis
The comedian who famously teamed up with singer Dean Martin still has a solo act in town.

2 Howard Hughes
The eccentric billionaire used his inheritance to make still more money in the film and airline industries before becoming a force in gambling.

3 Liberace

Wladziu Valentino Liberace – aka Mr Show Business – opened at the Riviera in 1955 and never looked back.

4 Clara Bow

Silent film star Clara Bow, who became known as the "It Girl," lived in Las Vegas with actor husband Rex Bell.

5 Wayne Newton

In 1957, 15-year-old Newton started at the Fremont; he is still performing in Las Vegas today.

6 André Agassi

Born in Las Vegas in 1970, Agassi rose to become one of the world's greatest (and most popular) tennis players.

7 Debbie Reynolds
The film star was also owner of a hotel-casino and museum of Hollywood memorabilia.

8 Robert Goulet
The actor/entertainer was a veteran of such hit Broadway musicals as *Carousel* and *The Man from La Mancha*.

9 Surya Bonaly
The former women's figure-skating champion now performs professionally.

10 Phyllis McGuire
The entertainer is fondly remembered as one of the singing McGuire Sisters.

For the top casinos See pp36–7

Left **The Venetian** Center left **New York–New York** Center right **Caesars Palace** Right **Excalibur**

🔟 Theme Hotels

1 The Venetian

Whether or not the Venetian really evokes accurate images of Venice is beside the point: the sum of the hotel's parts adds up to an aesthetically pleasing whole. (See pp20–21).

2 Caesars Palace

Caesars Palace opened in 1966 and was long the Strip's most opulent and, some would say, most ostentatious hotel. Times change, though, and Caesars recently was forced to put millions of dollars into renovations in order to keep up with new-comers. Cleopatra's Barge – a floating lounge – is still as it was, and the cocktail goddesses still wear toga-like cos-tumes, but new statues have been erected on the front lawn, and the former show theater, Circus Maximus, has been updated. ⓢ 3570 Las Vegas Blvd S. • Map P1–2 • 800 634 6001 • www.caesars.com • $$$$
(for price categories see p89)

3 Mandalay Bay

With its theme of Southeast Asia, Mandalay Bay has lush tropical foliage, dotted with tiny pagodas and temples. The huge swimming complex as well as sev-eral of the shops and the popular "rumjungle"

Hard Rock Hotel

restaurant and lounge (see p42) emphasize the theme. There is also an events center (see p40) and the House of Blues concert venue. ⓢ 3950 Las Vegas Blvd S. • Map R1–2 • 877 632 7000 • www.mandalay-bay.com • $$$

4 New York–New York

The Statue of Liberty raises her torch over the busiest inter-section in Las Vegas. Nearby the Empire State, CBS, and Chrysler buildings rub shoulders with the Brooklyn Bridge, Grand Central Station, and the New York Public Library. Despite the architectural license, New York–New York is an exciting place with all manner of well-observed details.
ⓢ 3790 Las Vegas Blvd S. • Map R1–2 • 888 696 9887 • www.nynyhotelcasino.com • $$

5 Hard Rock Hotel

The huge guitar sign outside and an enormous chandelier with

Performance of *The Sirens of TI*

saxophone pendants clearly identify this as a Hard Rock enterprise. Throughout the public rooms are displays of rock-and-roll memorabilia. And you'll hear only one kind of piped music, of course. ⊗ 4455 Paradise Rd • Map Q3 • 702 693 5000 • www.hardrockhotel.com • $$$

TI
This lavish hotel features a pool with private cabanas, gaming rooms, and an oversized hot tub for up to 25 people. Free nightly performances of *The Sirens of TI* are packed with daring swordplay, high-diving acrobatics, and pyrotechnics. Visitors can buy TI and Cirque du Soleil souvenirs in the shopping arcade. A pedestrian bridge connects the hotel with the Fashion Show Mall *(see p52)*. ⊗ 3300 Las Vegas Blvd S. • Map P2 • 702 894 7111 • www.treasureisland. com • $$$

Planet Hollywood
Vegas goes Hollywood at this stunningly ultra-modern resort and casino conveniently located near the center of the Strip. The 2,600 movie-themed rooms will appeal to film fans, while the vibrant dining and nightlife options attract a trendy crowd. There is also a spa, two swimming pools, and 1,500-seat theater. ⊗ 3667 Las Vegas Blvd S. • Map Q2 • 866 919 7472 • www. planethollywood.com • $$$

Paris Las Vegas
Alas, the City of Light has to lose something in translation to the City of Bright Lights. Even so, the Eiffel Tower model is impressive; the bicycle-riding delivery boy, and a cheery "bonjour" from valet-parking attendants are nice

Paris Las Vegas

touches, too. ⊗ 3655 Las Vegas Blvd S. • Map Q2 • 702 946 7000 • www. caesars.com/paris/lasvegas • $$$

Circus Circus
As its name suggests, this hotel-casino contains the world's largest permanent circus, as well as an indoor, 5-acre theme park. *(See p71.)*

Circus Circus

Excalibur
One of the first theme hotels (built in 1990), this is still a favorite with children. The legend of King Arthur and his Knights is the theme through the games arcade and on into the wedding chapel on the "Fantasy Faire" floor. ⊗ 3850 Las Vegas Blvd S. • Map R1–2 • 702 597 7777 • www.excaliburcasino.com • $$

Left **Arizona Charlie's** Center **Fiesta Rancho** Right **Harrah's Las Vegas**

TOP 10 Casinos

Rio
Cocktail waitresses in bright, flouncy costumes, an upbeat color theme, and friendly personnel make this casino a favorite with residents and visitors alike. The Rio also has the reputation of serving the best casino food in town. Video poker is the most popular game here, perhaps because mini-TV sets are mounted on top of some of the machines. *3700 W. Flamingo Ave • Map C4 • 800 752 9746 • www.harrahs.com*

Monte Carlo
The building reflects its European namesake, but the casino is typically Las Vegas, with the usual machines and table games. Monte Carlo's slot club is, however, superior to most; the air seems fresher than in most casinos, too. *3770 Las Vegas Blvd S. • Map Q2 • 800 311 8999 or 702 730 7777 • www.monte-carlo.com*

Monte Carlo

J. W. Marriott Las Vegas
The casino at this sophisticated Southwestern-style resort is small. It is also relatively quiet. Best of all, when gamblers want a break, they have a choice of strolling through the lush gardens, eating at eight different restaurants, and browsing the smart shops. *221 N. Rampart Blvd • Map A3 • 702 869 7777 or 877 869 8777 • www.marriott.com*

Santa Fe Station
People who suffer from claustrophobia in casinos will find relief here, where ceilings are high and small groups of machines are located near the entrance. An extensive remodeling program has added more parking, state-of-the-art race and sports betting facilities, and new restaurants, including Salt Lick BBQ. *4949 N. Rancho Drive • Map A1 • 702 658 4900 or 866 767 7771 • www.stationcasinos.com*

Harrah's
One of the most respected names in the gaming industry, Harrah's has more than a dozen properties across the USA and offers value for money in service, food, and ambience. Harrah's also has one of the best slot clubs as far as prizes are concerned; the club card can be used at any Harrah's casino, so it works well for people who like to gamble wherever they vacation. *3475 Las Vegas Blvd S. • Map P2 • 702 369 5000 • www.harrahs.com*

Loews Lake Las Vegas

Because of the hotel's location, 17 miles from Las Vegas, most of the people who gamble here are hotel guests, so it is usually quiet during the day when many of them are playing golf. Even when full, the casino never feels crowded – a great plus for people with a low tolerance for noise. ✆ *101 Montelago Blvd • Map H4 • 702 567 6000 • www.loewshotels.com*

The Golden Nugget, Fremont Street

Fiesta Rancho

The decor is unmemorable, but the slot and video-poker machines are considered the most liberal in town. There's a drive-up sports book – gamblers can place bets without getting out of their cars. Eateries are close to the casino floor, so non-stop gamblers don't have to take much time out for eating. ✆ *2400 N. Rancho Drive • Map B2 • 702 631 7000 • www.fiestacasino.com*

Golden Nugget

This casino sets itself apart from its downtown neighbors, for both clientele and ambience. The restaurants are very good, and the casino is a pleasant place to gamble while waiting to see the Fremont Street Experience *(see p79)*, which takes place just outside its doors. ✆ *129 E. Fremont St • Map K4 • 800 846 5336 • www.goldennugget.com*

Sunset Station

Primarily patronized by local residents, Sunset Station is located across from the Galleria at Sunset shopping mall. The casino is light and well-ventilated. It also has a Kids' Quest (nursery) on the premises. ✆ *1301 W. Sunset Rd, Henderson • Map F6 • 702 547 7777 • www.stationcasinos.com*

Sunset Station

Arizona Charlie's

Western-themed Arizona Charlie's is best known for its huge bingo parlor. There's also an enormous race and sports-book facility. It depends largely on the local trade, and its employees are very friendly. ✆ *740 S. Decatur Blvd • Map B3 • 702 258 5200 • www.arizonacharlies.com*

Left *Les Folies Bergère* Center *KÀ* Right *Blue Man Group*

Shows

"O"

"O," staged by Cirque du Soleil, is a circus quite unlike any other. The whole show revolves around the theme of water (hence the name, as in the French *eau*). The acrobats, synchronised swimmers, divers, and characters perform in, on, and above water. Seven hydraulic lifts raise and lower the water levels throughout the performance, allowing for spectacular diving and other feats. ◈ *Bellagio, 3600 Las Vegas Blvd S. • Map Q1–2 • 702 796 9999 for tickets*

Cirque du Soleil's "O"

Mystère

Created especially for TI, *Mystère* is an enchanting circus that – like all Cirque du Soleil productions – has a mystical thread running through it. The costumes are innovative and colorful, and together with the high-energy acrobatics, evocative dances, and vivid lighting an overwhelming sensory experience is created. ◈ *TI, 3300 Las Vegas Blvd S. • Map P2 • 702 796 9999 for tickets*

Lance Burton: Master Magician

Even people who don't usually care for magic shows wax lyrical about this one. Not only is Burton engaging, but his tricks are truly impressive. Children love this show: Burton invites them onto the stage to help him work his magic. The Victorian-style theater, designed especially for the show, is modeled on similar ones in London's West End. ◈ *Monte Carlo, 3770 Las Vegas Blvd S. • Map Q2 • 702 730 7160*

KÀ

This innovative theatrical spectacle from Cirque du Soleil features astonishing acrobatic performances, martial arts, puppetry, multimedia, and pyrotechnics. The colorful and entertaining show was inspired by the Egyptian belief in the "kà", an invisible spiritual body which accompanies a person

Mystère, TI

For more on shows See pp118–19

throughout their life. This theme is developed into an exciting tale about imperial twins who undertake a perilous journey into mystical lands. They face many challenges that must be overcome before can they fulfil their destiny. With astonishing computer-generated effects and 80 outstanding performers, the stage is brought to life in a blaze of fire and fantasy. ⬧ *MGM Grand, 3799 Las Vegas Blvd S. • Map R2 • 702 891 7777 or 1800 929 1111 (toll free) • www.ka.com*

Danny Gans

The award-winning master of impressionism has moved from The Mirage to the Encore Suites *(see p22)*. This multi-talented singer, comedian, and actor has been named Las Vegas' "Entertainer of the Year" for ten straight years in a row. His phenomenal repertoire includes 300 voices. ⬧ *Encore Suites at Wynn Las Vegas, 3131 Las Vegas Blvd S. • Map R2 • 702 770 9966*

Jubilee

Jubilee features showgirls who not only look good but also dance well. The show offers an effective mix of production numbers and specialty acts, glamorous costumes, and pretty tunes. There are terrific special effects, too, such as the sinking of the *Titanic*. ⬧ *Bally's, 3645 Las Vegas Blvd S. • Map Q2 • 702 946 4567*

Blue Man Group

Unique, funny, and wildly innovative, three bald blue men take the audience on a multi-sensory journey, featuring theater, percussion music, and vaudeville. Like nothing else you have ever seen! ⬧ *The Venetian, 3355 Las Vegas Blvd S. • Map R1 • 1800 258 3626*

Jubilee, Bally's

The Beatles LOVE

Cirque du Soleil combines its magic with the exuberant spirit and timeless music of one of the most-loved bands in the world. ⬧ *The Mirage, 3400 Las Vegas Blvd S. • Map P1–2 • 702 791 7111*

Les Folies Bergère

The longest running show in Las Vegas began in 1979, a century after the Paris production hit the stage. Like the original, the Vegas show is predicated upon glamorous showgirls wearing spangles, sequins, and little else. The production numbers are lavish, the music tuneful. While the first show each evening is suitable for families, the second is topless. ⬧ *The Tropicana, 3801 Las Vegas Blvd S. • Map R2 • 702 739 2417*

STOMP OUT LOUD

An exhilarating show in which the performers create melodious and rhythmic sounds from unusual objects. A loud, heart-pumping, feet-tapping treat for audiences of all ages ⬧ *Planet Hollywood Resort and Casino, 3667 Las Vegas Blvd S. • Map Q2 • 702 785 5555*

 For free entertainment **See p76**

Left **Thomas & Mack Center** Center **Le Théâtre des Arts** Right **Judy Bayley Theater**

🔟 Music and Performing Arts Venues

1 Hollywood Theater and Grand Garden Arena

Headliners such as Tom Jones and David Copperfield, and music acts such as Donny and Marie Osmond, regularly appear at the 630-seat Hollywood Theater *(below)*. MGM's larger 15,200-seat special-events center, the Garden Arena, is used for superstar concerts, major sporting events, and other spectaculars. It was the setting for the much-publicized Barbra Streisand Millennium Concert on New Year's Eve 1999, for which tickets cost as much as $2,500. ❀ *MGM Grand Hotel, 3799 Las Vegas Blvd S. • Map R2 • 800 646 7787*

2 Mandalay Bay Events Center

Luciano Pavarotti inaugurated the 12,000-seat events center in 1999. Since then, performers as diverse as tenor Andrea Bocelli (with the Russian Symphony Orchestra), Ricky Martin, and Bette Midler have graced its stage. During one month in particular, the Mandalay Bay Center was exceptionally eclectic, staging as it did a heavyweight bout between Evander Holyfield and John Ruiz, skater Katarina Witt's *Kisses on Ice* show, and Bocelli's vocal performance. ❀ *Mandalay Bay, 3250 Las Vegas Blvd S. • Map R2 • 702 632 7777*

3 The Showroom at Planet Hollywood

The 1,500-seat theater at Planet Hollywood Resort and Casino *(see p33)* has been remodeled for the resident show STOMP OUT LOUD. Previously, the venue was famous for productions such as *Forever Swing*, the Broadway musical *Fosse*, and *Les Misérables*. ❀ *Planet Hollywood Resort and Casino, 3667 Las Vegas Blvd S. • Map Q2*

4 Sam Boyd Stadium

The stadium hosts some of the biggest entertainment and sporting events in the country. Built in 1971, the seating capacity has been increased over the years: 40,000 spectators can now be accommodated. ❀ *University of Nevada Las Vegas, 7000 E. Russell Rd • Map F5 • 702 895 3900*

5 Judy Bayley Theater

In addition to possessing excellent acoustics and comfortable seats, the Judy Bayley Theater features a special stage of flexible design. Primarily used for ballet, musical comedy, and dramatic productions, the theater also serves as home to the Nevada Dance Theater. ❀ *University of Nevada Las Vegas, S. Maryland Parkway • Map Q4 • 702 895 ARTS*

For more on entertainment See pp118–19

Artemis Ham Concert Hall

Across the courtyard from the Judy Bayley Theater, the Artemis Ham Concert Hall is an elegant building that serves as the venue for performances of both nationally and internationally acclaimed musicians and dancers. Violinist Itzak Perlman and the Bolshoi Ballet are among the star names that have appeared here. ✪ *University of Nevada Las Vegas, S. Maryland Parkway • Map Q4 • 702-895-ARTS*

Thomas & Mack Center

Named for two leading bankers who financed the project, Thomas & Mack's gala grand opening in 1983 was nothing if not star-studded, featuring as it did Frank Sinatra, Dean Martin, and Diana Ross. The center serves as the venue for rodeos, university basketball games, circuses, world championship boxing matches, and concerts. The record box-office takings for a single event was $18 million for the Holyfield vs Lewis heavyweight boxing bout in 1999; the record attendance for a single concert was 17,664.
✪ *University of Nevada Las Vegas, S. Maryland Parkway • Map Q4 • 702 895 ARTS*

Orleans Showroom

The 800-seat theater presents several headliners each month. The list of performers is a veritable "who's who" of the entertainment world of yesteryear: Jerry Lewis; Willie Nelson; Peter, Paul, and Mary; Roy Clark; the Righteous Brothers; and Crystal Gayle, to name but a few. ✪ *Orleans Hotel, 4500 W. Tropicana • Map B4 • 702 365 7111*

Le Théâtre des Arts

The Parisian-style theater opened in 1999 and has already welcomed some big names, including Dennis Miller, Bobby Vinton, Earth, Wind, and Fire, and the Moody Blues. In 2008, it hosted the Broadway production of *The Producers*. ✪ *Paris Las Vegas, 3655 Las Vegas Blvd S. • Map Q2 • 877 374 7469*

Clark County Amphitheater

This outdoor amphitheater is the setting for a popular and eclectic range of free public entertainment, from "Jazz in the Park" and moonlight concerts to folk festivals and barbershop quartets. The amphitheater's "brown-bag" lunches attract workers from nearby office buildings, Las Vegas residents, and visitors alike. ✪ *500 S. Grand Central Parkway • Map K3 • 702 455 8200 • Events listed in local press*

Clark County Amphitheater emblem

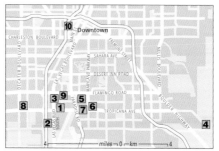

For free entertainment **See p76**

Left **Studio 54 dancers** Center **eyecandy sound lounge** Right **Pure at Caesars**

🔟 Nightclubs and Lounges

1 TAO Nightclub

The original TAO, a celeb-filled Asian bistro in New York, gets a Vegas makeover at The Venetian *(see pp20–21)*. Water-falls, giant Buddha statues, and an artificial sandy beach are the major features of this Asian-themed club. On Saturday nights the beach is transformed into an exotic night-spot, complete with a light show and floating Chinese lanterns in the pool. Famous guest DJs spin tunes on Sun-day nights. Drink at one of the three bars or enjoy the magnifi-cent views from the terrace. 🌐 *The Venetian, 3377 Las Vegas Blvd S. • Map P2 • 702 388 8588 • 5pm–12am Mon–Wed, 5pm–4am Thu–Fri, 5pm–4am Sat, 5pm–12am Sun • Admission charge*

Ghostbar

2 Studio 54

Like its Manhattan name-sake, Studio 54 attracts celebri-ties. Some of them even make impromptu stage appearances. There are four dance floors and bars, video displays, and live dancers, while special theme nights cater for different tastes. You can mostly expect to hear chart-topping dance hits. Semi-private lounge areas and VIP seating are available. 🌐 *MGM Grand, 3799 Las Vegas Blvd S. • Map R2 • 702 891 7254 • Open from 10pm Tue–Sat • Admission charge*

3 Drai's

Book-lined Drai's is Las Vegas's only after-hours club. A fireplace, comfortable upholstered chairs, and potted palms add to the intimate atmosphere. With some of the world's greatest DJs playing everything from techno to Latin rhythms, the party usually goes on well after sunrise. 🌐 *Bill's Gamblin' Hall & Saloon, 3593 Las Vegas Blvd S. • Map P2 • 702 737 0555 • Open from 1am Thu–Sun*

4 rumjungle

At 11pm, rumjungle converts from a restaurant to a nightclub. Live bands are accompanied by dancers and gymnasts. It has the world's largest rum bar. 🌐 *Mandalay Bay, 3950 Las Vegas Blvd S. • Map R1–2 • 702 632 7408 • Admission charge*

Studio 54

For more on live music See pp40–41

rumjungle

eyecandy sound lounge
A unique and visually stunning bar in the center of Mandalay Bay's main casino. A kaleidoscope of colors enlivens everything from the curtains to the dance floor. ✪ Mandalay Bay, 3950 Las Vegas Blvd S. • Map R1 • 702 632 7777 • Open 6pm–4am daily

Tryst
This hip nightclub is located in one of Las Vegas' mega resorts in the center of the Strip. Dress is casual chic, and definitely no hats, oversized jeans, or athletic wear allowed. European bottle service is required for reserved tables. ✪ Wynn Las Vegas, 3131 Las Vegas Blvd S. • Map N2 • 702 770 3375 • Open 10pm–4am Thu–Sun • Admission charge

JET
This spacious and luxurious nightclub features three distinct rooms and three dance floors each with a separate sound system, which caters for a variety of musical tastes. ✪ Mirage, 3400 Las Vegas Blvd S. • Map P1 • 702 792 7900 • Open 10:30pm–4am Fri–Sat, Mon • Admission charge

Pure at Caesars
A three-level, mega-club owned by, among others, Andre Agassi, Steffi Graf, and Céline Dion. It features an upscale VIP service and attracts some of the Strip's most stylish crowds. Opulent, oversized beds ring the main dance floor, while a huge outdoor terrace provides great views. ✪ Caesars Palace, 3570 Las Vegas Blvd S. • Map P1 • 702 731 7873 • Open 10pm–4am Fri–Sun

Body English at Hard Rock
The Hard Rock's signature nightspot is a riot of rocker chic with its grand staircase and crystal chandeliers. Leather booths line the club's two levels for those who need a break from the dance floor. ✪ Hard Rock Casino and Resort, 4455 Paradise Rd • Map Q3 • 702 693 4000 • Open 10:30pm–4am Wed, Fri–Sun • Admission charge

Ghostbar at Palms
One of the city's most futuristic and stylish nightspots, Ghostbar is best known for its "ghost deck" with its unforgettable views some 55 floors above the hotel pool. Attracts a young crowd. ✪ Palms, 4321 Flamingo Rd W. • Map B4 • 702 942 6832 • Open 8pm–3am nightly • Admission charge

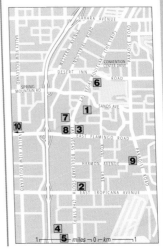

Left **Madame Tussaud's** Center **Las Vegas Natural History Museum** Right **Bellagio Gallery of Fine Art**

Museums and Galleries

Bellagio Gallery of Fine Art

This world-class gallery presents temporary exhibitions of nineteenth- and twentieth-century artworks and objects drawn from inter-national collections. A reduction in the admission charge in 2008 makes this an even better bargain. ◉ Bellagio, 3600 Las Vegas Blvd S. • Map Q1–2 • 702 693 7871 • Open 10am–6pm Sun–Thu, 10am–9pm Fri–Sat • Admission charge • www.bellagio.com

Madame Tussaud's Wax Museum

One can easily become so entranced with the wax figures that their theatrical settings are ignored (see pp28–9).

Lied Discovery Children's Museum

With more than 100 hands-on exhibits, this is one of the finest children's museums in the western USA. Children can

Pavarotti, Madame Tussaud's

learn about science, arts, and the humanities through entertaining games and workshops. There is an eight-story Science Tower for older children, and the little tots love the Bubble Pavilion and Toddler Towers. ◉ 833 Las Vegas Blvd N. • Map J5 • 702 382 3445 • Open 9am–4pm Tue–Fri, 10am–5pm Sat, noon–5pm Sun • Admission charge • www.ldcm.org

Liberace Museum

A fittingly flamboyant tribute to the king of kitsch. Don't miss the customized cars and pianos. Also on display are the trademark capes and sequined jackets, plus collections of objects from around the world, including a piano-shaped ring with 260 diamonds. ◉ 1775 E. Tropicana Ave • Map R5 • 702 798 5595 • Open 10am–5pm Tue–Sat, noon–4pm Sun, closed Mon • Admission charge • www.liberace.org

Lied Discovery Children's Museum

For more children's activities See pp66-7

Nevada State Museum and Historical Society

This outstanding institution aims to advance the understanding of the human and natural history of Nevada. Exhibitions include a fossil of the largest ichthyosaur ever found, and the arts and crafts of local Native Americans. ◈ 700 Twin Lakes Drive • Map J1 • 702 486 5205 • Open 9am–5pm daily • Admission charge • http://dmla.clan.lib.nv.us/docs/museums/lv/vegas.htm

Neon Museum

Where neon signs are seen as art. A fascinating and eclectic assemblage of outdoor signage that casts an illuminating glow on Las Vegas history. The signs in the collection date from the 1940s to the present day. ◈ Near 821 Las Vegas Blvd N. • Map D2–3 • 702 387 6366 • Tours by appointment only • Admission charge • www.neonmuseum.org

Las Vegas Natural History Museum

Highlights include the international wildlife room and a live shark exhibit. The children's hands-on exploration room is excellent, but the roars of the animated dinosaurs may elicit equally loud cries from frightened toddlers. ◈ 900 Las Vegas Blvd N. • Map J5 • 702 384 3466 • Open 9am–4pm daily • Admission charge • www.lvnhm.org

Clark County Heritage Museum

This unusual museum has historic buildings relocated from various sites around the state, as well as contemporary local artifacts.

◈ 1830 S. Boulder Hwy, Henderson • Map G6 • 702 455 7955 • Open 9am–4:30pm daily • Admission charge

Las Vegas Art Museum

Housed in a $20-million contemporary-style southwest building, the museum is a repository for both national and international works, with local arts and crafts in the gift shop. ◈ 9600 W. Sahara Ave • Map A3 • 702 360 8000 • 10am–5pm Tue–Sat; 1–5pm Sun

Marjorie Barrick Museum of Natural History

The fascinating exhibitions at this museum include the arts of the Southern Paiute, live reptiles of the Mojave Desert, and crafts from Mesoamerica. The Xeriscape is an attractive arboretum of drought-tolerant plants. ◈ UNLV Campus • Map Q4 • 702 895 3381 • 8am–4:45pm Mon–Fri, 10am–2pm Sat • Free

Dinosaur, Natural History Museum

Left **Rosemary's** Center **Joël Robuchon** Right **Pamplemousse**

Gourmet Restaurants

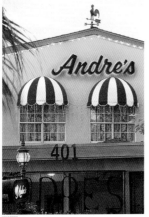

Andre's
Quintessentially French restaurant in a converted house. *Coquilles* St. Jacques, magret of duck, lobster sausage, and smoked goose breast are classics. Service is gracious, and Andre Rochat presides over the kitchen. ⊗ *401 S. 6th Street • Map K4 • 702 385 5016 • $$$$$ (for price categories see p90)*

Pamplemousse
With rough-hewn beams, baskets of fresh flowers on the tables, and nooks decorated with pottery and copper cookware, Pamplemousse ("grapefruit" in French) resembles a dining room in Provence. Dinner begins with a basket of fresh seasonal vegetables to create a custom salad.

Picasso

Entrées include veal medallions in a dijon-accented cream sauce, and roast duckling in a red wine and rum sauce. ⊗ *400 E. Sahara Ave • Map M3 • 702 733 2066 • $$$$$*

Picasso
The room is exquisite, with original Picassos on the walls and a carpet designed by Pablo Picasso's son, Claude, underfoot. Spanish-born chef, Julian Serrano, creates contemporary French dishes with an Iberian accent. Among the delights are filet of black bass, a warm lobster salad, sautéed foie gras, and pan-seared Nantucket scallops. ⊗ *Bellagio Hotel, 3600 Las Vegas Blvd S. • Map Q1–2 • 702 693 7223 • $$$$$*

Joël Robuchon
A feast for both the palate and the eyes, the food at this out-standing restaurant is predominantly French with Asian and Spanish influences. Signature dishes include fresh scallops with lemon and seaweed butter, and green asparagus with *Oscetra* caviar. ⊗ *MGM Grand, 3799 Las Vegas Blvd S. • Map R2 • 702 891 7925 • $$$$$*

Rosemary's
An extensive menu features the likes of rosemary roasted lamb with black olive mashed potatoes and grilled prime

For more great places to eat See pp48–9, 82, 90, 96 & 106

flat-iron steak with asparagus and prosciutto. Scrumptious desserts, include lemon ice-box pie with raspberry sorbet. The paintings on the walls are by local artists and are for sale. ◐ 8125 W. Sahara Ave • Map M1 • 702 869 2251 • $$$$

Chinois
If you read through the whole menu you may never get around to eating at Chinois – the sushi section alone lists 35 choices. Sizzling whole catfish and sweet soy-glazed Atlantic salmon are prepared with a French twist. ◐ Forum Shops at Caesars, 3500 Las Vegas Blvd S. • Map P1–2 • 702 737 9700 • $$$$

Prime Steakhouse at Bellagio
Superstar Chef Jean-Georges Vongerichten takes classic steakhouse dining to new heights. Veal porterhouse with kumquat and pineapple chutney, and caramelized cauliflower is a signature dish. ◐ Bellagio, 3600 Las Vegas Blvd S. • Map Q1 • 702 693 7111 • $$$$$

Chinois

Mon Ami Gabi at Paris Las Vegas
Menu highlights at this Baroque-style, authentic Parisian bistro include the onion soup, steak frites, and strawberry crêpes. There are breathtaking views of the Strip when dining alfresco on the terrace. ◐ Paris Las Vegas, 3655 Las Vegas Blvd S. • Map Q2 • 702 944 4224 • $$$$

Roy's
The innovative menu at this award-winning restaurant features Hawaiian fusion cuisine. The predominantly seafood dishes include wasabi crab stuffed

Prime Steakhouse

mushroom benedict, and fire-grilled yellow fin ahi. There is a large parking lot and a children's menu. ◐ 620 E. Flamingo Rd • 702 691 2053 • $$$$$

Bradley Ogden
Your tastebuds are in for a treat at the elegant restaurant of Bay Area chef Bradley Ogden. Ingredients are flown in daily to create innovative dishes, such as halibut with stuffed squash blossoms. Divine desserts. ◐ Caesars Palace, 3570 Las Vegas Blvd S. • Map P1-2 • 702 731 7410 • $$$$$

For restaurant price categories See p90

Left and center **Flavors Buffet** Right **Carnival World Buffet**

🔟 Salad Bars, Buffets, and Brunches

Village Seafood Buffet
This buffet was an instant success when it opened in 1997 and continues to be a favorite with local residents. Lobster tail, shrimp, clams, and other seafood are flown in fresh daily and kept fresh in saltwater; the seafood Mongolian barbecue is especially good. ⌖ *Rio Hotel, 3700 W. Flamingo Rd • Map C4 • 702 252 7777 • $$$*

Carnival World Buffet
Half the fun here is watching the chefs work as they interpret the flavors of Brazil, the East, Italy, Mexico, and the USA in a staggering 1,000-recipe repertoire. ⌖ *Rio Hotel, 3700 W. Flamingo Rd • Map C4 • 702 252 7777 • $$*

Sterling Brunch
This may be the most expensive brunch in town, but the Sterling Brunch can compete with any in the world for quality and imagination. Two dozen appetizer choices include prosciutto mousse on raspberries, caviar with warm blinis, and lobster gazpacho. Roast salmon in phyllo pastry with shrimp and spinach mousseline is the carving station star, while French toast with cinnamon ice cream provides a delicious finale. Reservations required. ⌖ *Bally's, 3645 Las Vegas Blvd S. • Map Q2 • 702 967 4661 • $$$$*

Bellagio Buffet
A large, sumptuous dining buffet offering more than 60 dishes, ranging from Chinese to Italian, and from Japanese to new American cuisine. Specialties include all the shrimps you can eat, wild duck breast, and roast venison. Save room for the decadent cheesecake or the heavenly chocolate-dipped strawberries. ⌖ *Bellagio, 3600 Las Vegas Blvd S. • Map Q2 • 702 693 7111 • $$$*

Sweet Tomatoes Salad Bar
The cool green and white interior plus extras like custom-made omelets and stuffed potato distinguish this salad bar from its rivals. The choice of dressings is extensive, and the ingredients are garden-fresh. The homemade chili is divine. ⌖ *375 N. Stephanie St • Map E6 • 702 933 1212 • Another branch at 2080 N. Rainbow Rd • 702 648 1957 • $*

Sweet Tomatoes Salad Bar

For more on eating out See pp82 & 90

Golden Nugget Buffet

Flavors Buffet

The Harrah's group of hotel-casinos has a reputation for excellent food. Although the buffet offerings at the Fresh Market Square are not as unusual as those of some competitors, the standards of preparation and service are consistently high. Folks in the know go for the salads and extremely attractive desserts. ◈ *Harrah's, 3475 Las Vegas Blvd S. • Map P2 • 702 693 6060 • $$*

The Buffet at TI

This attractive buffet features six live-action exhibition stations where a great selection of barbecued meats, Asian dishes, pasta, pizza, salads, and desserts are prepared. There is also a roving Chili Cart. ◈ *TI, 3300 Las Vegas Blvd S. • Map P2 • 702 894 7111 • $$*

Souper Salad

The murals of bountiful harvests along the wall sum up the big-eating philosophy of this chain of glorified salad bars. Help yourself to everything you can eat – soup, main-course salads, pasta, pizza, dessert – for an incredibly low $5.90. ◈ *4022 S. Maryland Parkway • Map P4 • 702 792 8555 • Another branch at 2051 N. Rainbow Blvd • $*

Golden Nugget Buffet

There are around 60 buffet rooms in Las Vegas, and most could not be described as aesthetically lovely. The setting of the Nugget, however, is just that. The dishes are pretty tasty, too: don't miss the fresh carved turkey and old-fashioned bread pudding. ◈ *Golden Nugget Hotel, 129 Fremont St • Map K4 • 702 385 7111 • $$*

Le Village Buffet

An innovative blend of offerings at the Paris Las Vegas Hotel, including omelets, imported cheeses, bouillabaisse, wild mushroom bisque, lamb, venison, prime rib steak, and huge shrimp, all followed by a wealth of French-inspired desserts. ◈ *Paris Las Vegas, 3655 Las Vegas Blvd S. • Map Q2 • 702 946 7000 • $$*

For price categories **See p91**

Left **Little Church of the West** Center **Couple at Viva Las Vegas** Right **Touting for business**

Wedding Chapels

Bellagio Wedding Chapels
Bellagio's two chapels provide some of the most elegant and romantic wedding venues in Las Vegas. Both have a stained-glass window behind the altar, while ornate lamps and chandeliers of amethyst and Venetian glass complement the pastel shades of the furnishings. Personalized services are available for room reservations as well as both wedding and reception planning.
Ⓢ *Bellagio, 3600 Las Vegas Blvd S. • Map Q2 • 702 693 7700, 888 987 3344*

Viva Las Vegas
Don't let the humble, rustic interior cramp your style: the chapel has a selection of fancy costumes at your disposal, covering such themes as Egyptian, Beach Party, Victorian, Gangster, Western, and even Intergalactic. Ⓢ *1205 Las Vegas Blvd S. • Map L3 • 702 384 0771*

Little Church of the West
The Little Church opened in 1942, making it one of the oldest wedding chapels in town. It is a favorite with the stars: Zsa Zsa Gabor and George Saunders, Betty Grable and band leader Harry James, and model Cindy Crawford and actor Richard Gere have all graced its portals.
Ⓢ *4617 Las Vegas Blvd S. • Map C5 • 702 739 7971*

Jewish Temples
Very few churches and synagogues – as distinct from wedding chapels – perform "walk-in" ceremonies. Marriage requirements vary from congregation to congregation. Contact Temple Beth Sholom or Temple Adat Ari El for more information. Ⓢ *Temple Beth Sholom (Conservative United), 10700 Havenwood Ln • 702 804 1333 • Map L4 • Temple Adat Ari El (Reformed), 4675 W. Flamingo Rd • 702 221 1230*

Christ Church Episcopal
This traditional Episcopal church is the closest one to the Strip. Bear in mind that churches in the Episcopal Diocese of Nevada require pre-nuptial meetings with the church's rector before a wedding can be performed. Ⓢ *2000 S. Maryland Parkway • Map M4 • 702 735 7655*

Guardian Angel Cathedral
Just steps away from the dazzling, bustling Strip, the Roman Catholic

Guardian Angel Cathedral

For more on getting married in Las Vegas See pp120–21

cathedral is refreshingly spartan. The giant triangular mosaic decorating the façade depicts a guardian angel and three figures representing Penance, Prayer, and – perhaps most elusive of all – Peace. ✆ *302 Cathedral Way • Map N2 • 702 735 5241*

Canterbury Wedding Chapels
Create your own version of Camelot by renting period costumes and tying the knot in one of Excalibur's two medieval-style chapels. Vow-renewal services are also on offer for the already-wed. ✆ *Excalibur, 3850 Las Vegas Blvd S. • Map R1 • 702 597 7278*

Island Wedding Chapel
Located at the Tropicana, this chapel offers wedding ceremonies in a tropical paradise. There are two options on offer – take your pick from a ceremony in the lush Polynesian Gardens Gazebo or the South Seas-style palm-thatched Chapel. The Island Wedding Chapel was voted lushest chapel in Las Vegas by *Brides Magazine* in 1999. ✆ *3801 Las Vegas Blvd S. • Map R2 • 702 798 3778 • www.tropicanachapel.com*

The Little White Chapel
This chapel represents what for many people is the epitome of Las Vegas; it has acquired a reputation for hosting rather unusual weddings. It was here in the spring of 2001 that a mass wedding took place, officiated by multiple Elvises. For the bride and groom who are acting on mad impulse or whose hectic lives leave them only a few minutes to spare, the Little White Chapel offers the world's only Drive-Up Wedding Window. The window never closes, and

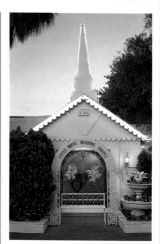

The Little White Chapel

no appointment is necessary. ✆ *1301 Las Vegas Blvd S. • Map L4 • 702 382 5943 • www.alittlewhitechapel.com*

Hot-air Balloon Ceremonies
A hot-air balloon company and The Little White Chapel collaborate to provide airborne weddings in winter. The balloon hovers above the Las Vegas neon while the nuptial knot is tied. ✆ *Little White Chapel in the Sky • 702 382 5943, 800 545 8111*

Left **Canal Shoppes** Right **Las Vegas Outlet Center**

TOP 10 Places to Shop

The Forum Shops at Caesars

The Forum Shops are laid out along pseudo-Roman streets within the Caesars Palace complex, characterized by two-story storefronts topped with statues of Roman senators. Along with wares from Europe, American design is featured at stores like Banana Republic, Ann Taylor, and Houdini's Magic Shop. Ask for a map of the shops at the Las Vegas Convention & Visitors Authority *(see p115)* before you put on your shopping shoes. *(See also pp26–7.)*

Via Bellagio

Simply walking along Via Bellagio *(see also p15)* is an unforgettable experience. The boutiques are so opulent as to be intimidating: even if you dare not step inside, then at least the entrances to Hermès, Chanel, Gucci, and others are large enough to see inside. Tiffany's windows are especially dazzling during the holiday season.
◈ *Bellagio, 3600 Las Vegas Blvd S. • Map Q1–2*

Miracle Mile

British fashion at French Connection, leisure wear at Urban Outfitters, and beautiful accessories at Pashmina by Tina are located here. Alternative merchandising comes from shops such as Tommy Bahama, which captures the *joie de vivre* of the tropics.
◈ *Within Planet Hollywood Resort and Casino, 3667 Las Vegas Blvd S. • Map Q2*

Fashion Show Mall

This upscale shoppers' paradise boasts Saks Fifth Avenue and Nordstrom department stores. The mall also hosts fashion shows and events. ◈ *3200 Las Vegas Blvd S. • Map N2*

The Galleria at Sunset

One of the city's residential malls, the Galleria at Sunset offers department store shopping and down-to-earth services, such as shoe and jewelry repair, free jewelry cleaning, alterations and tailoring, hairstyling, film developing, gift wrapping, and postage stamps. ◈ *1300 W. Sunset Rd, Henderson • Map E5*

Via Bellagio

For more on shopping **See pp54–5 & 116**

Las Vegas Top 10

6 Las Vegas Outlet Center

Internationally known brands such as Nike shoes and Calvin Klein clothing are among the almost 150 outlets in this ever-expanding mall. The discounts on goods can be astonishing – sometimes as high as 75 percent. Style-conscious parents should seek out the children's outfitters Oshkosh B'Gosh, Tommy Kids, and Carter's. The obligatory Vegas-style entertainment comes in the form of a giant carousel. ⊗ 7400 Las Vegas Blvd S. • Map C6

7 Canal Shoppes

Located on the second floor of the Venetian (see pp20–21), the emphasis at Grand Canal Shoppes is on European elegance. Exquisite goods for sale include handmade Venetian lace, glass, and masks as well as silks, shoes, and jewelry from various European countries. Part of the pleasure of shopping at this mall is the distinctive ambience – it may not be quite like the real Venice, but the experience is enjoyable nonetheless. ⊗ The Venetian, 3355 Las Vegas Blvd S. • Map P2

8 Mandalay Place

An eclectic selection of shops located on a 100,000-sq-ft (9,290-sq-m) sky bridge, connecting Mandalay Bay with the Luxor Hotel and Casino. Stores include the world's first Nike Golf store and LUSH PUPPY, the first pet boutique on the Las Vegas Strip. Plenty of restaurants and eateries as well. ⊗ Mandalay Hotel, 3950 Las Vegas Blvd S. • Map R1–2

9 Town Square Shopping Plaza

Take some time out from the Strip's sensory overload at this large outdoor mall with its village-like storefronts and quaint streetscapes. The 150-plus stores and restaurants include big-name favorites such as Gap, H&M, and Apple. There is plenty of entertainment with an 18-screen movie theater and a kids' playground, boasting a 42-ft (13-m) tall tree house. There is also a wide range of restaurants. ⊗ 6605 Las Vegas Blvd S. • Map C5

Town Square Shopping Plaza

10 The Shoppes at The Palazzo

The latest attraction for shoppers looking for luxury goods can be found within the Palazzo, part of the Venetian casino and hotel complex (see p21). The Shoppes feature more than 60 high-end stores, such as the specialty fashion emporium, Barneys New York. Other fashion brands of note include Michael Kors, Christian Louboutin, and Diane Von Furstenberg. ⊗ The Palazzo, 3325 Las Vegas Blvd S. • Map P2

Left **Dice clock** Center left **Circus Circus ornament** Center right **Vegas puzzle** Right **Elvis glasses**

🔟 Souvenirs

1 Jigsaw Puzzles of the Strip

A pastime with no cash payout, but plenty of variety in terms of styles of puzzle and images of Vegas. The most popular are puzzles that piece together the Strip by night or form cartoon renditions of sights along the Strip. And since this part of Las Vegas is ever-changing, you may one day have a collector's item.

2 Personalized Poker Chips

The perfect souvenir for people who host their own card games. Personalized chips come in traditional colors *(see p124)*, but can bear your name in place of a casino's name and logo.

Retro slot machine

3 Souvenir Photos

Have your picture taken dressed as a pioneer, a cowboy, or a showgirl. Or, if the fancy takes you, you can dress up in a medieval outfit. Alternatively, have your face substituted for a magazine-cover celebrity. The photos generally cost $25 or less and make fun mementos.

4 Elvis Sunglasses with Fake Sideburns

Although he didn't make much of a hit when he first appeared in Las Vegas in 1956, Elvis Presley has since been firmly associated with the Entertainment Capital of the World. Your career as an Elvis impersonator could start here, with a pair of these sunglasses and sideburns.

5 Dice-Decorated Clocks

Made of bright blue lucite, glittery gold plexiglass, brass, wood burls, or any other material known to man, these clocks – with dice marking the hours – fall into the genre of Las Vegas kitsch. Other tacky items include toilet seats inlaid with playing cards and poker chips, and tissue box covers with gaming motifs.

6 Books about Nevada

Las Vegas bookstores carry a large assortment of publications on the locale, including *The Nevada Trivia Book* by Richard Moreno, *A Short History of Las Vegas* by Myrick and Barbara Land, and several about slot machines by Marshall Fey (grandson of the inventor of the first slot machine). For fiction, try *Sweet Promised Land* or *A Cup of Tea in Pamplona* by the late Basque-American writer, Robert Laxalt.

7 Nevada-Made Gourmet Foods

The best-known Nevada-made edibles are Ethel M. Chocolates, created by Forrest Mars, a

Poker chips

member of the Milky Way, Mars, Three Musketeers, and M&Ms manufacturing family. For the more refined palate, try Mrs Auld's Sweet 'n' Spicy pickles, her scone mix, or brandied cherries; Davidson Teas are good, too.

Antique Slot Machines

Machines that date back to 1895 – when Charles Fey invented the very first slot machine, *The Liberty Bell* – occasionally appear on the auction block. Designs range from high Victoriana to Art Deco, and the rarer antique models can cost several thousand dollars.

Show Programs and Logo Items

Each major Las Vegas show has a shop associated with it, usually located near the box office. Commemorative T-shirts and various production recordings are the most common items for sale. However, anything that can be sold will be sold, including magicians' equipment, Chinese circus plates, and logo-emblazoned bottle stoppers, skipping ropes, and yo-yos.

Cash

The ultimate item to bring home from a Las Vegas trip has got to be several suitcases of hard cash. Although there are more losers than winners at the slot machines, roulette wheels, and gaming tables, visitors occasionally hit big jackpots, such as those on Megabucks and Quartermania machines, netting them huge sums of money.

Picture-Perfect Photo Spots

Bellagio Conservatory
Arrange your subjects in front of the most gorgeous floral display. The skylights give good light (see p15).

Venetian Gondola
Have someone in another gondola take the photo so you can be in it, too (see p20).

Hard Rock Hotel Swimming Pool
Best taken from a hotel room to get the pool's guitar shape (see pp32–3).

Terrace, Loews Lake Las Vegas
Wonderful at sunset, when the hills and houses are bathed in a gold light (see p37).

Madame Tussaud's
Have your loved one stand next to his or her favorite wax museum celebrity (see pp28–9).

Brahma Shrine, Caesars Palace
This lovely shrine is supposed to bring good luck (see p32).

TI Gangway
Either of the ships makes a delightful backdrop for your photos, or take a shot of the ships and village (see p33).

Glitter Gulch Entertainers
Pair your subject with a celebrity impersonator, who will be pleased to pose for a tip (see p13).

TI – Venetian Overcrossing
A great vantage point for photographing the Strip. ✆ Map P2

The Mirage Volcano
The 54-ft (16-m) high volcano at the Mirage is a Las Vegas landmark and a spectacular free show (see p73).

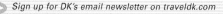

Left **The Roller Coaster** Right **Las Vegas Motor Speedway**

🔟 Thrill Rides and Simulators

1 The Roller Coaster

For those more thrill-seeking riders who dare to keep their eyes open during this white-knuckler, the Coney Island-style ride offers spectacular views of the Strip. The coaster route writhes, dips, dives, and loops around the resort's perimeter. ⊗ *New York–New York, 3790 Las Vegas Blvd S. • Map R1–2*

2 Big Shot

Located on the world's tallest observation tower, the Big Shot shoots riders 160 ft (50 m) into the air. They then freefall back to the launch pad. It's not a ride for the faint-hearted, or for kids – fortunately for them, though, there's a child-size version of Big Shot at Stratosphere. ⊗ *Stratosphere Tower, 2000 Las Vegas Blvd S. • Map L–M3*

3 The Desperado

Billed as one of the fastest roller coasters in the U.S., The Desperado reaches speeds of up to 80 mph (129 kph). Try to catch the great views of the Primm Valley from the highest point. If that isn't enough of a thrill, try falling 170 ft (52 m) on the Turbo Drop or get drenched on the Adventure Canyon Log Flume. ⊗ *Buffalo Bill's, 31900 Las Vegas Blvd S., Primm Valley, 35 miles (56 km) south of Las Vegas on I-5 • Map T2 • 702 679 7433 • Age, height, and weight restrictions*

4 Pole Position Raceway

This state-of-the-art race-kart facility offers a driving opportunity for beginners and experts alike. Celebrity sightings are common. ⊗ *4175 South Arville • Map B4–5 • 702 227 7223 • Age, height, and weight restrictions*

Big Shot, Stratosphere

Share your travel recommendations on traveldk.com

Canyon Blaster

5 There are some fun rides to sample at Adventuredome, Circus Circus' indoor theme park. Possibly the most exciting ride is the high-speed

Indoor Skydiving

Canyon Blaster, which is billed as "the only double-loop, double-corkscrew indoor roller coaster." Disk-O is a dual rocking and spinning ride accompanied by loud disco music. Riders should expect a soaking on the Rim Runner water-flume ride. ✪ *Circus Circus, 2880 Las Vegas Blvd S. • Map M–N3*

Roller coaster, Sahara Speedworld

Sahara Speedworld

6 Surely the closest one gets to being launched into outer space without actually doing it. The "slingshot" electronic technology launches passengers on "Speed," the aptly named roller coaster. A 360-degree loop and a vertical climb of a 225-ft (68-m) tower (both forward and backward) add to the excitement – and it's all over in 48 seconds. ✪ *Sahara Hotel & Casino, 2535 Las Vegas Blvd S. • Map M3*

Magic Motion Machines

7 The exciting, but short, motion rides inside Excalibur include "Sponge Bob Square Pants 4D," where you journey under the sea, and "Corkscrew Hill," a simulated medieval adventure. ✪ *Excalibur, 3850 Las Vegas Blvd S. • Map R1–2*

Zero G

8 The ultimate ride if cost is no object. For $3,950 plus tax, experience weightlessness in a Boeing 727. The four-hour journey begins with 90 minutes of flight training, then it's up into the sky in G-Force One for a series of dives to achieve zero gravity. Photos and DVD are included in the cost. ✪ *5275 Arville Street • Map B5 • Age and medical restrictions apply*

Indoor Skydiving

9 Flyaway Skydiving advises potential customers that skydiving is not without risk. The experience includes training and a simulated skydive in a wind tunnel. ✪ *Flyaway Indoor Skydiving, 200 Convention Center Drive • Map N3*

Richard Petty Driving Experience

10 After instruction, participants get into the driver's seat of an authentic Winston Cup-style stock car, and go, go, go! ✪ *Las Vegas Motor Speedway, 6975 Speedway Blvd • Map E1*

For more activities for children **See pp66–7**

Left **Powerboat racing, Lake Mead** Right **National Finals Rodeo**

🔟 Festivals and Annual Events

1 Chinese New Year
Chinese New Year festivities center around Chinatown Plaza *(see p85)*. Highlights include the traditional Chinese lion dance, firecrackers, foods, and *feng shui* as it pertains to the New Year. ✪ *Chinatown Plaza, Spring Mountain Rd • Map B4 • Late Jan–mid-Feb*

2 St. Patrick's Day Celebration
St. Patrick's parties are held at various restaurants and bars, with the main celebration at the Fremont Street Experience *(see p79)*. Crowd-pleasers include the Las Vegas Highland Pipe Band, entertainment on two stages, green beer (with green food coloring), and traditional Irish dishes. ✪ *Map K4 • Mar 17 or closest weekend*

3 Cinco de Mayo
The Mexican national holiday commemorating the victory of the Mexicans over the French in 1862 is celebrated by the entire Las Vegas Hispanic community, including people from Central America and Cuba. Bands play everything from *ranchero* to rock. *Piñatas, mariachis*, carnival rides, and games, as well as food vendors selling *tamales*, tacos, and flan add to the festivities. ✪ *Freedom Park • Map D2 • May 5 or closest weekend*

4 Snow Mountain Powwow
Tribal dancers in costumes decked out with beadwork, bones, shells, and bells come from across North America to perform ritual dances handed down from their ancestors. Feathered shields and foods such as Navajo tacos and fry bread are sold. ✪ *Paiute Indian Reservation, 30 miles N • 702 658 1400 • May*

5 Clark County Basque Festival
Events during this festival pertaining to all things from the Basque culture of northern Spain include a Catholic mass; feats of strength such as chopping huge logs in half and carrying heavy weights; and traditional dancing. Basque food is in abundance, and the *picon* punch is potent. ✪ *St. Viator Community Center, 4320 Channel 10 Drive, Clark County • 702 361 6834 • Sep*

6 Pacific Islands Festival
The many Pacific Rim peoples who live in the Las Vegas area celebrate their various heritages one day each year with continuous entertainment, cultural exhibits, and fashion boutiques. Food includes everything from *kim-chee* and *poi* to potstickers and teriyaki. ✪ *Lorenzi Park, 333 W. Washington Ave • Map C2 • 702 382 6939 • Sep*

Tournament golf

7 Halloween Haunted Houses

A group of professional magicians create haunted houses in parking lots, community centers, and parks. The "Texas Screamer" haunted house comes complete with mad doctor's laboratory and a surprise visit from the Texas chainsaw lunatic. ◊ *Late Oct*

8 Strut Your Mutt

No matter their pedigrees – or lack thereof – every dog has his day when the Strut Your Mutt competition takes place. There's the Mutt Parade and competitions to find the best dressed dog, the one with the most spots, and the one who can do the silliest tricks. ◊ *Dog Fanciers' Park, 5800 E. Flamingo Rd • 702 455 8206 • Nov*

9 National Finals Parties and BBQ Cook-Off

During the National Finals Rodeo, all of Las Vegas seems to go country – wearing jeans and boots. Casinos bring in country music bands, and line-dancing is enacted. The venues change from year to year, including that of the barbecue cook-off. The free entertainment magazines are the best sources of information about what's going on where. ◊ *Various venues • Dec*

10 Festival of Trees and Lights

Opportunity Village, an organization that helps the mentally challenged, raises funds by creating a Magical Forest with 50 decorated Christmas trees. The centerpiece is Santa's Castle, fashioned by the toy wizards FAO Schwarz. ◊ *Opportunity Village, 6300 W. Oakey Blvd • 702 259 3700 • Throughout Dec*

Sporting Events

1 National Finals Rodeo
Cowboys compete for millions of dollars in prize money at the USA's premier rodeo. ◊ *Thomas & Mack Center • early Dec*

2 World Championship Boxing
Las Vegas is now the premier city for title bouts. ◊ *Caesars Palace, MGM Grand, Mandalay Bay, Thomas & Mack Center*

3 NASCAR Winston Cup Series
The Winston West motorcar race. ◊ *Las Vegas Motor Speedway • Dates vary*

4 Baseball
Watch the Las Vegas 51s on their home ground. ◊ *Cashman Field, 850 Las Vegas Blvd N. • Apr–Labor Day*

5 UNLV Sports Events
The university's Runnin' Rebels basketball, football, and baseball teams are frequently champions. ◊ *Thomas & Mack Center • Sep–May*

6 NHRA Summit Nationals
Dragsters battle for supremacy. ◊ *Las Vegas Motor Speedway, 7000 Las Vegas Blvd N. • Apr*

7 World Series of Poker
Poker players compete for $1 million. ◊ *Rio Suites Hotel • Apr–May*

8 PBR Championship
Professional bull-riding competition. ◊ *Thomas & Mack Center • Last weekend in Oct*

9 Las Vegas Cup Powerboat Racing
Boats in various classes compete for prizes. ◊ *Lake Mead • Jun*

10 Las Vegas Invitational Golf Tournament
Famous for being Tiger Woods' first PGA championship. ◊ *Various courses • Mid-Oct*

Left **Jet skiing** Right **Cycling at Desert Shores**

🔟 Outdoor Activities

1 Hiking at Red Rock Canyon

Follow Hwy 159 (Charleston Boulevard) west for about 25 minutes to find yourself in another world in the Red Rock Canyon National Conservation Area *(above)*. A scenic drive loops through Red Rock Canyon: venture off this to get away from civilization *(see pp24–5)*.

2 Cycling at Desert Shores

Cycling in Las Vegas can be pleasant – especially in the quieter, smarter residential areas of Green Valley and off Charleston Boulevard. Even better, though, are the paths at Desert Shores, in northwest Las Vegas, where you'll enjoy abundant shade and water views.

3 Jet Skiing on Lake Mead

Water babies should head for Calville Bay Marina or the Lake Mead Marina to rent jet skis, water skis, and other water craft. Note that the wearing of life jackets is obligatory out on the water. *(See pp92–5)*.

4 Roller-Blading at Summerlin

Summerlin is a planned community northwest of downtown, and its smooth sidewalks are perfect for roller-blading. The surroundings are among the most pleasant in the city, generally smog-free with attractive houses and condominiums. In-line hockey fans should head for the rink at the Sports Park. ⊙ *Las Vegas Sports Park, 1400 N. Rampart Blvd*

5 Tennis at Sunset Park

The eight floodlit courts at Sunset Park *(below)* are easy to get to (they are only about a mile from the southern end of the Strip), and they also cost far less than the courts at sports clubs and hotels. While you wait for a court enjoy the ringside view of

For more on hiking **See p108**

planes coming in to land at McCarran International Airport. ✪ Map D5 • 702 455 8200

6 Skiing and Snowboarding at Mt. Charleston

Although the snow can't compare with that at famous resorts such as Aspen, Colorado, the skiing at Mt. Charleston can be surprisingly good and makes a fantastic contrast to golf and swimming in the valley below. Ski lessons and equipment rentals are available in the Lee Canyon Ski Area, which is off Hwy 156. ✪ 45 miles (72 km) NW of Las Vegas • 702 645 2754 • www.skilasvegas.com

Ball games in Sunset Park

7 Swimming at Northwest Pool

Although almost every hotel and motel in Las Vegas has a swimming pool, people who want to swim laps may find that there are too many other swimmers in the way. For a good pool workout, locals head for the eight-lane Northwest Pool. When you're bored with doing laps (or your children are bored with you doing laps), there is a 178-ft (54-m) spiral slide and an aquatic play gym. ✪ 8601 Gowan Rd

8 Outdoor Basketball

There always seem to be pick-up basketball games in progress at either Desert Breeze Park or Sunset Park. The former has only two courts, but they are very new and of good quality. ✪ Desert Breeze Park, 8275 Spring Mountain Rd • Sunset Park • Map D5

9 Strolling the Strip

Although there are dozens of paths off the beaten track, such as those at Arroyo Grande Park in Green Valley, most Las Vegas visitors do their strolling along the world-famous Strip. And why not? This road, actually a 3.5-mile (6-km) section of Las Vegas Boulevard South (or Hwy 604) is one of the most fascinating highways in the world. ✪ Map M3–R2

10 Jogging at Sunset Park

If you're up to more than just a casual stroll down the Strip, one of the most popular joggers' venues is Sunset Park. Paths are well maintained and the circuit includes a fitness course. And there's plenty to look at to keep your mind off your feet: disc-golf courts, horseshoe pits, volleyball, and radio-controlled boating on the park's lake. ✪ Map D5

For activities for children See pp66–7

Left **Las Vegas National Golf Club** Right **Angel Park Golf Clubs**

🔟 Golf Courses

1 Reflection Bay Golf Club

Nominated frequently by golf magazines as one of the top 10 courses in the USA, Reflection Bay, designed by the great Jack Nicklaus, follows 1.5 miles (2.5 km) of the Lake Las Vegas shoreline. Great views of the lake and million-dollar hillside homes are an added bonus. Ⓢ *75 Monte Lago Blvd, Henderson • Map H4 • 702 740 4653*

2 The Legacy Golf Course

The host to the US Open Qualifying tournament is a popular course with convention delegates, and combines Scottish links-style golf with the dramatic desert vegetation of Nevada *(below)*. The course highlight is the Devil's Triangle (holes 11–13). Ⓢ *130 Par Excellence Drive, Henderson • Map E6 • 702 897 2187*

3 DragonRidge Golf Course

With its manicured fairways, bent-grass greens, and dramatic elevation changes, DragonRidge offers some of the most spectacular views in the valley. The course is private, with limited public play. Ⓢ *552 S. Stephanie St, Henderson • Map E6 • 702 614 4444*

4 Bali Hai Golf Club

Just steps away from the Mandalay Bay and Four Seasons hotels, the course features thick stands of palm trees, large water hazards, tropical plants, and flowers in its South Seas design *(above)*. Ⓢ *5160 Las Vegas Blvd and Russell Rd • Map C5 • 702 450 8000*

5 Angel Park Golf Clubs

The Palm and the Mountain, this club's two 18-hole championship layouts designed by legendary American golfer Arnold Palmer, have been described as the "world's most complete golf experience." A night-lighted driving range, 18-hole putting course, and golf school form part of the complex. Ⓢ *100 S. Rampart Blvd • Map A3 • 702 254 4653*

Angel Park

6 Las Vegas Paiute Resort

This was the first master-planned multicourse golf resort on Native American land. The Snow and Sun Mountain courses were designed by Pete Dye, who has designed 11 of the world's top 100 courses. ⊗ *Snow Mountain, Highway 95 (exit 95), 25 miles (40 km) N of Las Vegas* • *702 658 1400*

7 Desert Willow Golf Club

This challenging course is carved from the foothills of the Black Mountains and surrounded by hazards and hilly terrain. ⊗ *2020 W. Horizon Ridge Parkway, Henderson* • *702 270 7008*

8 Las Vegas National Golf Club

Established in 1961, this was the scene of champion Tiger Woods' first PGA (Professional Golf Association) victory in the 1996 Las Vegas Invitational. Soft spikes are preferred (some Las Vegas courses prohibit spikes of any kind). ⊗ *1911 E. Desert Inn Rd* • *Map D4* • *702 734 1796*

9 Royal Links Golf Club

The course features holes inspired by famous holes on the Open courses in Great Britain. All the golf carts are equipped with GPS (Global Positioning Systems). ⊗ *5995 E. Vegas Valley Blvd* • *Map E4* • *702 450 8000*

10 The Revere at Anthem

Winding through three desert canyons, this course features natural changes in elevation and spectacular views of the Las Vegas skyline. The summer rates, as at many Las Vegas courses, are considerably lower than those charged at other times of the year. ⊗ *2600 Hampton Rd, Henderson* • *702 259 4653*

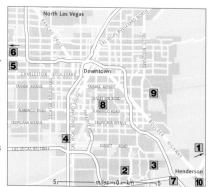

For more outdoor activities **See pp60–61**

Left **Stone massage** Right **The Spa at Ceasars Palace**

🔟 Spas and Health Clubs

Canyon Ranch Spaclub
Residents at the Venetian can enjoy the 100-plus spa services, including movement therapy and 20 different styles of massage. The huge facility is also open to non-residents, as is the Canyon Ranch restaurant. 🔊
The Venetian, 3377 Las Vegas Blvd S. • Map P2 • 702 414 3600

Aquae Sulis Health Spa
Named for the Roman baths and settlement at what is now the city of Bath, England, this luxurious spa's traditions are rooted in the benefits of ritual bathing and body treatments. Choose simply to "take the waters" or indulge in a Southwestern hot-stone massage. East Indian Siddha Vaidya therapies are also offered. 🔊 *J. W. Marriott Hotel, 221 N. Rampart Blvd • Map A3 • 702 869 7807*

Kim Vō Salon, Spa at The Mirage

The Spa at The Mirage
Feel your stresses and strains ebb away at this beautifully redesigned spa with its calming, neutral decor. There are additional treatment rooms and a more indulgent menu. Celebrity colorist, Kim Vō, has opened a salon just next door, including a barber shop for men. 🔊 *The Mirage, 3400 Las Vegas Blvd S. • Map P1–2 • 702 791 7474*

The Spa at Caesars Palace
With a style that recaptures the glorious splendor that was ancient Rome, the spa incorporates Roman baths and other touches of imperial luxury. In addition to the myriad treatments on offer for both men and women, there are weight-training facilities, a fitness center with climbing wall, and a yoga studio. 🔊 *3570 Las Vegas Blvd S. • Map P1–2 • 702 731 7776*

Drift Spa
Dark stones and sleek furnishings set the scene for a chic relaxation experience at Drift Spa. A rejuvenating menu is based on the traditions of Turkey, Tunisia, Morocco, and Spain. Couples especially will delight to find treatment rooms featuring private gardens. Other enticing features include hot and cool soaking pools, a traditional co-ed Turkish Hammam, and private outdoor garden lounges. 🔊 *Palms Place, 4381 West Flamingo • Map C4 • 702 944 3219*

For more on hotel facilities **See pp14–15, 20–23 & 32–3**

Spa at Monte Carlo

Topline furnishings from across the globe and personalized service are hallmarks of this spa, which has a cozy and intimate atmosphere. Heliotherapy, body wraps, body scrubs, facials, and a variety of

Spa Bellagio

massages are on the menu of services. ◈ *Monte Carlo, 15 Las Vegas Blvd • Map Q2 • 702 730 7590*

MGM Grand Spa

Pamper yourself with a "Dreaming Ritual" package, which offers a foot soak, massage, and mud therapy treatment set to Aboriginal music. You can purchase day passes for the workout room, sauna, and jacuzzi. There's also a top hair salon overlooking the pool. ◈ *MGM Grand, 3799 Las Vegas Blvd S. • Map R2 • 702 891 3077*

Spa Bellagio

This Italianate pampering palace combines the elegance of marble with cutting-edge fitness equipment. The spa's signature treatment is the Bellagio Stone Massage, which combines specially "harvested" stones prepared in a hydrobath with an energy-balancing technique to provide a thoroughly relaxing experience. Service is attentive. ◈ *Bellagio, 3600 Las Vegas Blvd S. • Map Q1–2 • 702 693 7472*

The Spa at New York-New York

It will take far longer than a New York minute to enjoy all that is on offer at this revamped spa. Relaxing treatments include the Long Island Getaway Scrub, New York Minute Manicure, and the Traffic Stopper Facial. ◈ *New York-New York, 3790 Las Vegas Blvd S. • Map R1-2 • 702 740 6955*

Las Vegas Athletic Club

The Athletic Club is considered by Las Vegas residents to be one of the premier fitness facilities in the city. It contains all the usual gym equipment, plus virtual-reality exercise machines, abdominal and cardio rooms, and childcare facilities. The rates are reasonable, too, and the surroundings scrupulously clean. ◈ *2655 S. Maryland Pkwy • 702 734 5822*

Left **Old West theme park, Bonnie Springs** Right **Rainbow Theatre**

Children's Attractions

Adventuredome
This indoor amusement park has an extensive array of rides and games designed to keep kids entertained for hours. They can ride the Canyon Blaster, a looping roller coaster, or get wet on a water flume ride, Rim Runner. *Circus Circus, 2800 Las Vegas Blvd S. • Map M2–N2 • 702 794 3939 • Open daily, hours vary • Admission charge*

Siegfried & Roy's Secret Garden and Dolphin Habitat
These two attractions come as a package, combining education and entertainment. Watch the dolphins *(right)* from above then use the tunnel for underwater viewing. The Secret Garden is an oasis of trees and greenery, with unusual residents, including a snow leopard, black panthers, Bengal tigers, and rare white lions. You are allowed to stay as long as you like. *The Mirage, 3400*

Dolphin Habitat, Mirage

Las Vegas Blvd S. • Map P1–2 • 702 791 7111 • Open 11am–5:30pm daily (Secret Garden closes 3:30pm daily) • Free for children under 10; admission charge for others

Rainbow Theatre
Children will find the dramatizations of folk tales, children's classic plays, musical comedies, and fantasies such as *No One Will Marry a Princess with a Tree Growing Out of Her Head* absolutely riveting. Performances of several works are presented each year. *821 Las Vegas Blvd N. • Map J5 • Programs vary • 702 229 6553 • Admission charge*

Interactive Fountains
Quarter-size holes in a plaza at this residential shopping center unexpectedly spurt out water at regular intervals throughout the day. Bring your youngsters dressed in their bathing suits so they can play while you relax on the café terraces. *Green Valley town center, 4500 E. Sunset Rd • Map E5 • Free*

SoBe Ice Arena

SoBe ice rink offers both figure skating and ice hockey facilities, as well as skate rental and lessons. *Fiesta Rancho Casino Hotel, 2400 N. Rancho Drive • Map B2 • 702 647 7465 • Admission charge*

6 Las Vegas Mini Gran Prix

Adult Gran Prix Cars, sprint karts, go karts, kiddie karts, plus the Dragon Coaster, Super Slide, and lots of arcade games make this a favorite off-Strip destination for Las Vegas kids as well as visitors. ✪ *1401 N. Rainbow Blvd • Map A2 • 702 259 7000 • Open 10am–10pm daily (to 11pm Fri & Sat) • Admission charge*

7 Southern Nevada Zoological Park

Nevada's only zoo features a collection of animals indigenous to the state, and a few domestic animals that can be seen up close. The zoo is also home to a family of rare Barbary apes, as well as many other mammals, birds, and reptiles. Kids are sure to love the petting zoo. ✪ *1775 N. Rancho Rd • Map J1 • 702 647 4685 • Open 9am–5pm daily • Admission charge*

8 Bonnie Springs and Old Nevada

This Old West theme park, which is 45 minutes west of the Strip, may lack the slickness typical of others in Las Vegas, but its rough-and-ready charm usually wins the children over. Among the best features are staged gunfights, stagecoach rides, a zoo, and stores with merchandise from the days of yore. ✪ *Gunfighter Lane, nr Red Rock Canyon • 702 875 4191 • Open 10:30am–5pm daily (to 6pm May–Sep) • Admission charge*

9 Orleans Bowling Center

Las Vegas has a lot of bowling alleys, but the Orleans, which has no fewer than 70 lanes, is consistently voted the

Lion enclosure, MGM Grand

favorite in the annual newspaper poll. Reasons for its success include the spacious surroundings, numerous tables and chairs, a state-of-the-art computerized scoring system, and a snack bar with a big choice of items. ✪ *Orleans Hotel, 4500 W. Tropicana Avenue • Map B4 • 702 365 7400 • Open 24 hours • Admission charge*

10 MGM Grand Lion Habitat

The pampered cats are bathed, dried, and groomed daily before being transported to the enclosure at the MGM Grand. Few children can resist the lure of baby animals, and lions are very special. When the cubs are old enough to leave their mothers, they can be watched in a special "nursery" where they play with toys – and with the humans who feed and care for them. ✪ *MGM Grand, 3799 Las Vegas Blvd S. • Map R2 • Open 11am–10pm daily • Free*

Following pages **Heart of the Strip**

LAS VEGAS TOP 10

Left **Circus Circus** Center **Tower, The Venetian** Right **Fountains, Bellagio**

The Strip

WALK ALONG THE LAS VEGAS STRIP and you'll see that some of the best things in Las Vegas life are free – especially when it comes to sightseeing and entertainment. It costs nothing to walk through the hotel-casinos, and you can window-shop to your heart's content in their shopping promenades. The hotel architecture makes for an attraction in its own right: where else would you find an Egyptian sphinx, a Polynesian paradise, and a medieval castle in the same block? In addition, some hotel-casinos have free entertainment going on outside their doors.

Circus Circus

The Sirens of TI

Strip Sights

1 The Sirens of TI
2 Circus Circus
3 Fountains at Bellagio
4 MGM Grand Lion Habitat
5 The Luxor
6 The Forum Shops at Caesars
7 Imperial Palace Auto Collection
8 Shark Reef at Mandalay Bay
9 Paris Las Vegas
10 The Mirage Volcano

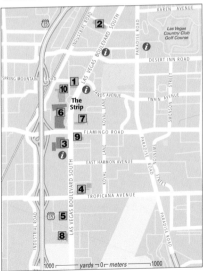

Gondoliers, The Venetian

The Sirens of TI

This free show, staged in a cove built at the entrance to TI, is a favorite with visitors to Las Vegas. The 23-minute crowd-pleaser showcases the beguiling and beautiful "Sirens of TI", who tempt and lure a band of swashbuckling pirates. From lively sword fights and acrobatic feats of derring-do to dazzling pyrotechnics and a rousing song-and-dance finale, this show is a hit, drawing huge crowds to their evening performances.
⊗ *TI, 3300 Las Vegas Blvd S. • Map P2 • Performances spring & summer: 7pm, 8:30pm, 10pm, & 11:30pm daily; winter & fall: 5:30pm, 7pm, 8:30pm, & 10pm daily • Free*

Circus Circus

Over the course of almost 30 years, Circus Circus has entertained hundreds of thousands of spectators with their impressive shows. Stars have included the Flying Farfans of Argentina, the miniature-bicycle rider Charles Charles of Paris, and Russian acrobat Valerie Akishin. With perform-ances taking place every half hour, you can pop back for different shows and catch a wide variety of acts.
⊗ *2880 Las Vegas Blvd S. • Map M–N2 • Performances every half hour, 11am–midnight • Free*

Fountains of Bellagio

More than 1,000 fountains perform a water ballet above Lake Bellagio, in defiance of the parched, baking desert that surrounds the city. Soaring as high as 240 ft (73 m) in the air, the cascading water is choreo-graphed to classical music. Bellagio and the other properties in the MGM MIRAGE group use incandescent lighting rather than neon, which make the Italian village surrounding the lake a lovely backdrop for the dancing waters. ⊗ *3600 Las Vegas Blvd S. • Map Q1–2 • Performances every half hour, 3pm–8pm Mon–Fri, 12pm–8pm Sat–Sun. Every 15 mins 8pm–midnight daily • Free*

MGM Grand Lion Habitat

In keeping with MGM's lion theme *(below)*, the hotel has a glass viewing enclosure, allowing you to stand face to face with the king of beasts. The lions, when not in the habitat, live in custom-built accommodations on an 8.5 acre (3.5 hectare) ranch 12 miles (20 km) from the hotel. ⊗ *MGM Grand, 3799 Las Vegas Blvd S. • Map R2 • Open 11am–10pm • Free*

➡ *For more on shows See pp38–9*

Auto Collection at the Imperial Palace

The Luxor

A strikingly modern twist on an ancient classic, the Luxor's unique 30-floor, black-glass pyramid is one of the most recognizable landmarks in Vegas. A life-size replica of the Great Temple of Ramses II is prominently featured inside the awe-inspiring atrium, which at 29 million cubic ft (820,000 cubic m) is one of the largest in the world. A 10-story sphinx (larger than the Egyptian original) guards the premises. The Luxor is also home to Cirque du Soleil production, CRISS ANGEL Believe, and BODIES... The Exhibition. ◈ *Luxor Hotel & Casino, 3900 Las Vegas Blvd • Map R1 • 702 262 4000*

The Forum Shops at Caesars

Listen in on conversations between the robotic statues of Bacchus, Venus, Pluto, and Apollo at the Festival Fountain *(below)*, and watch a mini-drama

performed by another group of statues – Neptune and his feuding children – at the Atlantis Monument between the Cheesecake Factory and Race for Atlantis. The show also features huge winged beasts and a dazzling, hi-tech wrath-of-the-gods firestorm. Some of the shops, too, provide entertainment: pop into Magic Masters and look out for a secret door leading to the replica of Harry Houdini's library. *(See also pp26–7.)*

Auto Collection at the Imperial Palace

Perhaps the most fascinating aspect of this collection is that all the vehicles (more than 250) are for sale. Elvis Presley's 1972 Lincoln Continental and a 1965 Rolls Royce Silver Cloud III that was once owned by Lucille Ball are just two of the vehicles that have passed through these doors. Look out for free tickets at tourist-information stations and in entertainment magazines. ◈ *Imperial Palace, 3535 Las Vegas Blvd S. • Map P2 • 702 794 3174 • Open 9:30am–9:30pm daily • Admission charge*

Shark Reef at Mandalay Bay

It is truly awe-inspiring to wander within the special walkways of the 1.3 million-gallon (5.9 million-liter) aquarium and observe the thousands of weird and wonderful sea creatures swimming together. Look out for the arowana dragon fish – and, of course, 11 different species of shark. ◈ *Mandalay Bay, 3950 Las Vegas*

Blvd S. • Map R1 • Open 10am–11pm daily • Admission charge

Paris Las Vegas

The Eiffel Tower and Arc de Triomphe are faithfully and impressively reproduced at Paris Las Vegas Hotel, albeit on a smaller scale than the originals. Buy fresh baguettes from a street vendor, and nibble to the strains of tunes by the great Maurice Chevalier, as interpreted by a wandering accordionist. ◈ 3655 Las Vegas Blvd S. • Map Q2

The Mirage Volcano

With displays like this, it is hardly surprising that the Mirage, when it was built in 1989, is said to have triggered the 1990s hotel-building boom. The man-made, multimillion-dollar volcano (below) spews fire 100 ft (30 m) into the air every 15 minutes, every evening. Ingenious lighting and steam effects convey the drama of lava flows, while loudspeakers broadcast vivid sound effects. ◈ The Mirage, 3400 Las Vegas Blvd S. • Map Q1 • Erupts 7pm–midnight • Free

A Day on the Strip

Morning

Start with breakfast in the delightful Verandah Café at Four Seasons, which is within **Mandalay Bay**. While there, visit **Shark Reef** where you'll be glad you're not about to become one of their specimen's breakfast. Also within the hotel is the **House of Blues**, worth checking out for the excellent collection of American folk art.

Head north up the Strip to the **Lion Habitat** at **MGM Grand** (p71) followed by a walk to the **Auto Collection at the Imperial Palace** (car buffs may have to be removed forcibly!).

For lunch, cross over to Harrah's for the **Fresh Market Square Buffet** (see p49).

Afternoon

At the **Forum Shops** you are liable to shed the shoppers in your party.

Next stop is **Circus Circus** (see p71). It's a hike, so you may opt for the CAT bus or monorail that stop along the Strip. After your trip there, you deserve a sugar break. Head for the Krispy Kreme doughnut shop and enjoy one of their legendary doughnuts. Newly fortified, explore Circus Circus (laugh at your stomach outline in the funhouse mirrors) and then walk back down to **TI** and watch **The Sirens** show.

Cross the street to Casino Royale, get a window table, and watch **The Mirage Volcano** erupt while you dine. For a nightcap, walk down to the Eiffel Tower at **Paris Las Vegas**, for the best view of **Fountains of Bellagio** (see p71).

For more information on getting around Las Vegas See p114

Price Categories

For a standard, double room per night (with breakfast if included), taxes, and extra charges.

$	under $50
$$	$50–$100
$$$	$100–$150
$$$$	$150–$200
$$$$$	over $200

Above **Caesars Palace**

Hotels

The Big Theme Hotels
The four largest and most extravagant hotels are Bellagio *(See pp14–15)*, The Venetian *(pp20–21)*, Mandalay Bay *(p32)*, and Paris *(p33)*. Smaller than these, but still extraordinary in their dedication to a theme, are Caesars Palace *(p32)*, New York – New York *(p32)*, TI *(p33)*, and Excalibur *(p33)*.

Tropicana
Island music, exotic birds, and waterfalls make this complex a tropical paradise. ◎ *3801 Las Vegas Blvd S. • Map R2 • 800 634 4000 • www.tropicanalv.com • $$$*

Harrah's
Friendly hotel with comfortable rooms. It is also possible to play keno through the room's TV set. ◎ *3475 Las Vegas Blvd S. • Map P2 • 800 427 7247 • www.harrahs.com • $$$*

Circus Circus
A vast property with child-friendly attractions. ◎ *2880 Las Vegas Blvd S. • Map M–N2 • 800 634 3450 • www.circuscircus.com • $$*

Bally's
This hotel has a relaxed atmosphere, an olympic-size swimming pool, and large, luxurious rooms, many with good views of the Strip. ◎ *3645 Las Vegas Blvd S. • Map Q2 • 800 634 3434 • www.ballyslv.com • $$*

Las Vegas Hilton
Elvis Presley is the star most associated with this hotel, appearing here for 837 sold-out performances. The luxurious suites have classic themes. ◎ *3000 Paradise Rd. • Map N3 • 702 732 5111 • www.lvhilton.com • $$$$$*

Mirage
Conveniently located in the center of the Strip, the Mirage is famous for its tropical atrium, pretty pool with cascading waterfall, and Siegfried & Roy's white tigers. ◎ *3400 Las Vegas Blvd S. • Map P1–2 • 702 791 7111 • www.themirage.com • $$$$*

Monte Carlo
An elegant European theme is reflected in the large rooms, each with a marble bathroom. ◎ *3770 Las Vegas Blvd S. • Map Q1–2 • 800 311 8999 • www.monte-carlo.com • $$*

MGM Grand
Despite being one of the largest hotels in the world, the Grand maintains a relaxed ambience. It boasts a luxurious spa *(See p65)*. ◎ *3799 Las Vegas Blvd S. • Map R2 • 800 929 1111 • www.mgmgrand.com • $$$*

Luxor
Its 30-story pyramid and giant sphinx have been Vegas landmarks since 1993. ◎ *3900 Las Vegas Blvd S. • Map R1 • 800 288 1000 • www.luxor.com • $$*

For more theme hotels See pp32–3

Left **MGM Grand Arcade** Center **Gameworks** Right **Coney Island Emporium**

🔟 Game Arcades

1 Fantasy Faire
Traditional carnival attractions take on a new excitement in a resort featuring medieval knights racing around on their steeds. ⊗ *Excalibur, 3850 Las Vegas Blvd S. • Map R1*

2 Gameworks
Perhaps the noisiest place in town, Gameworks occupies a vast space on the lower level of the Showcase Mall, and offers more than 250 games as well as a restaurant and climbing wall. ⊗ *3785 Las Vegas Blvd S. • Map R2*

3 Tropicana Arcade
Located just off the pool, this arcade is superbly convenient for parents who want to cool off while their children enjoy more than 30 games on offer. ⊗ *Tropicana, 3801 Las Vegas Blvd S. • Map C4–5*

4 Caesars Garden of Games
In this strange juxtaposition of ancient Rome and modern Las Vegas, techno-warriors do battle amid fluted columns with sophisticated arcade games. ⊗ *The Forum Shops at Caesars, 3500 Las Vegas Blvd S. • Map P1–2*

5 MGM Grand Arcade
The arcade features a great range of video and virtual-reality games. ⊗ *MGM Grand, 3799 Las Vegas Blvd S. • Map R2*

6 Sports Zone
Extreme sports are the attraction in this constantly supervised arcade. A Pizza Hut Express provides snacks. ⊗ *Las Vegas Hilton, 3000 Paradise Rd • Map N3*

7 Midway at Circus Circus
Games galore, plus an array of fun mirrors, hotdog stands, popcorn machines, and other carnival delights. ⊗ *Circus Circus, 2880 Las Vegas Blvd S. • Map M–N2*

8 Coney Island Emporium
Try out Big Apple-themed versions of traditional games such as coin pitches and shooting galleries, with New York-style food close at hand. ⊗ *New York–New York, 3790 Las Vegas Blvd S. • Map R2*

9 Monte Carlo Arcade
This arcade seems less hectic than most – a boon to anxious parents watching over their charges. ⊗ *Monte Carlo, 3770 Las Vegas Blvd S. • Map Q1–2*

10 In-Room Video Games
Most major Strip hotels will rent or loan video-game equipment to guests with children. Since by law no child under the age of 12 should be left unsupervised in a game arcade (and there is also a curfew for under-18s), many parents want to take advantage of this useful service.

⟶ For more on activities for children See pp66–7

75

Left *The Sirens of TI* Right *The Forum Shops, Caesars Palace*

🔟 Free Entertainment

The Sirens of TI
Top of the bill is the spectacular siren show staged in the evening at the hotel entrance (see p71). 🅢 *TI, 3300 Las Vegas Blvd S. • Map P2*

Caesars Palace Grounds
When Caesars Palace opened in 1966, no one had ever seen anything quite like it. The grounds, studded with Roman-style statuary, were – and still are – enchanting. 🅢 *Caesars Palace, 3570 Las Vegas Blvd S. • Map P1–2*

Paris Las Vegas
It may not be *quite* the real thing, but well-observed touches lend the place a characteristic joie de vivre (see p73). 🅢 *Paris Las Vegas, 3655 Las Vegas Blvd S. • Map Q2*

The Venetian's Gondoliers and Minstrels
The gondoliers sing as they pole their boats, and when not on the water they roam the casino harmonizing Italian arias. 🅢 *The Venetian, 3355 Las Vegas Blvd S. • Map P2*

MGM Grand Lion Habitat
A unique and impressive display in honor of the symbol of MGM (see p71). 🅢 *MGM Grand, 3799 Las Vegas Blvd S. • Map R2*

Mirage Volcano
This is Las Vegas at its lavish best: after dark, every 15 minutes, the "volcano" at the Mirage blows its top (see p73). 🅢 *The Mirage, 3400 Las Vegas Blvd S. • Map P1–2*

Silverton Aquarium
Just a short drive from the Strip is a vibrant, living sea. More than 5,000 exotic marine species live in this 117,000-gallon (440,000-liter) saltwater aquarium. 🅢 *Silverton Hotel and Casino, 3333 Blue Diamond Rd • Map B6–C6*

Fountains of Bellagio
The breathtaking choreography of the fountain displays at Bellagio offers some of the best free entertainment in Las Vegas (see p71). 🅢 *Bellagio, 3600 Las Vegas Blvd S. • Map Q2*

M&Ms World
Extraordinary as it seems, an entire attraction – including a 3-D movie – has been built around these tiny, candy-coated chocolates. 🅢 *Showcase Mall, 3875 Las Vegas Blvd S. • Map Q2*

The Sphinx at Luxor
It would be a shame (if hard) to miss the 10-story sphinx (larger than the original) guarding the Luxor Hotel-Casino (see p72). The best view of this landmark is as you come in to land at McCarran International Airport. 🅢 *Luxor Hotel, 3900 Las Vegas Blvd S. • Map R1*

For more free entertainment See p82

Left **Mirage Volcano** Center **Fountain show, Bellagio** Right **MGM Grand's fiber-optic sign**

🔟 Places to People-Watch

Bellagio Lobby
Settle down on a sofa to watch the gold dripping from the jet set. Soothe your envy with piano music from the caviar bar, Petrossian, and the marvelous artistry of the ceiling. ✪ *Bellagio, 3600 Las Vegas Blvd S. • Map Q1*

Benches at Miracle Mile
Too much shopping is bad for the feet. So sit yourself down on one of those inviting benches in Miracle Mile at Planet Hollywood, and watch the world go by; the best ones are near Cashman Photos. ✪ *Planet Hollywood, 3667 Las Vegas Blvd S. • Map Q2*

Around the Casino Tables
The stars play at upscale casinos such as MGM Grand, Bellagio, and Caesars Palace; stargazers should aim, apparently, for 11pm to 1am on weekends.

Mon Ami Gabi
Take a table at the sidewalk café, soak up the atmosphere, and enjoy the view of Bellagio's fountain show. ✪ *Paris Las Vegas Hotel, 3655 Las Vegas Blvd S. • Map Q2*

TI, Venetian, and Bellagio–Bally's Footbridges
Hop across Las Vegas Boulevard without playing traffic roulette, and enjoy marvelous vantage points of the mêlée below. ✪ *Map P2–Q2*

Bodies . . . The Exhibition
Explore the beauty of the human body. This exhibit at the Luxor *(see p72)* is dedicated to illustrating the wonders of our own bodies. It will inspire a curiosity and awe. ✪ *Luxor, 3900 Las Vegas Blvd S. • Map C5*

Film Locations
Do some detective work on where the stars are each day by calling 702 486 2727. This number will tell you the daily casting calls and where filming is taking place.

Fiber-Optic Signs
An increasing number of supersize signs like the one at MGM are appearing on the Strip. Look up at one of these to gain a new perspective on your fellow men. ✪ *MGM Grand, 3799 Las Vegas Blvd S. • Map R2*

Studio 54
Serious star-hunters should book a table at Studio 54 nightclub *(see p42)* as it's not unusual to spot celebrities enjoying a dance here. ✪ *MGM Grand, 3799 Las Vegas Blvd S. • Map R2*

Forum Shops at Caesars
The cafés and benches within the shopping complex are good for relaxation and people-watching *(see pp26–7)*. ✪ *Caesars, 3500 Las Vegas Blvd S. • Map P1–2*

Left **Glitter Gulch lights** Right **Pawn Shop Plaza**

Downtown

THE LAS VEGAS DOWNTOWN *is not a place of megastory financial temples. Instead, it is a conglomeration of government buildings, carnival attractions, not-so-very-glamorous casinos, storefront shops dealing in souvenirs, and unclaimed pawn shop miscellany.*
Glitter Gulch is the heart of the area, with its neon-lit row of casinos and, since the mid-1990s, free entertainment in the form of the Fremont Street Experience. This nightlife zone is here to stay, but the Las Vegas leadership is also planning a legitimate downtown on 61 acres close to Fremont Street, which will reflect the status of Las Vegas as one of America's richest cities.

Left **Fremont Street Experience** Right **Old Las Vegas Mormon Fort Historic Park**

🔟 Downtown Sights

1. Glitter Gulch
2. Fremont Street Experience
3. Downtown Casinos
4. View from Stratosphere Tower
5. Old Las Vegas Mormon Fort Historic Park
6. Pawn Shop Plaza
7. Bonanza Gift Shop
8. Vegas Vic Sign
9. World's Largest Slot Machine, Four Queens
10. Jackie Gaughan's Plaza Hotel-Casino Railroad Station

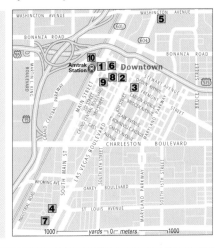

Glitter Gulch

The area called Glitter Gulch encompasses about eight blocks that front on Fremont Street between Main and Fourth streets. Along this stretch is the most concentrated dazzle of neon on the planet. Not only are all the Fremont

Stratosphere Tower

Street casino fronts decorated with neon, but the street signs and light shows *(see p82)* above contribute to the sparkling brilliance. Nighttime, of course, is when the lighting is at its most intense. The crowds on the malled walkway are heavy until after midnight, and the entertainment adds to a feeling of carnival. *(See also pp12–13.)*

Fremont Street Experience

The part of Fremont Street associated with Glitter Gulch is now under cover and the site of lavish free entertainment collectively labeled the Fremont Street Experience. Alongside spectacular nightly sound and light shows *(see p82)*, special events take place throughout the year, such as the March St. Patrick's Day Celebration, Pride Parade in May, Las Vegas Culture Fest in September, a Veterans Day Parade in November, and the Holiday Festival in December. ◈ *Fremont St betwen Main and 4th • Map K4*

Downtown Casinos

Along with all the outdoor activity on Fremont Street, there's action inside the casinos, too. They may not be as glamorous as the big hotels on the Strip, but the Fremont Street and other

downtown clubs have more history – some date back to the 1940s. They are also known for their bargain meals.

View from Stratosphere Tower

You may not be able to see forever exactly but, from the top of the tower on a clear day, parts of Arizona and California come into view. Count the 40 seconds it takes for the high-speed elevators to whiz up to the tower's floor-to-ceiling glass observation floor, which is 900 ft (275 m) above street level. The tower is a tourists' after-dark favorite for viewing the mesmerizing lights of Glitter Gulch and along the Strip. ◈ *2000 Las Vegas Blvd S. at the corner of Main St • Map M3 • Free*

Old Las Vegas Mormon Fort Historic Park

Mormons built the fort, along with a trading post in 1855, as a defense against the Native Americans (who turned out to be peaceful). It is the oldest building of its type in Nevada, but of the original structures only a small adobe building that was part of the stockade remains. ◈ *500 Washington Ave E. • Map J5 • Open 8:30am–4:30pm daily, except Christmas through New Year's Day • 702 486 3511 • Admission charge*

⬎ *For more on Glitter Gulch* **See pp12–13**

Glitter Gulch, with the illuminated icon, Vegas Vic

Pawn Shop Plaza

Chainsaws, boom boxes, fake Rolex watches, belt sanders, diamond rings, car jacks, and hundreds more items are piled on counters and hung from the ceilings in the shops of the plaza. This astonishing assemblage is testimony to the fact that some gamblers will sacrifice almost anything. Nevada law permits a monthly ten percent interest on pawn shop loans – few pledges are redeemed. ◈ *Area on First St north and south of the Fremont St intersection • Map J4*

Bonanza Gift Shop

The mother-of-all-souvenir-stores *(right)* includes such delights as miniature slot machine banks, X-rated bumper stickers, Elvis motifs on black velvet, sequin-studded hats, personalized dice, and gambling chip-encrusted toilet seats. The place is enormous, crowd-ed with tourists, and crammed with anything that can possibly be marketed as a souvenir of the city. ◈ *2460 Las Vegas Blvd S. • Map M3*

New Year's Eve in Glitter Gulch

Historically, Glitter Gulch has been the place favored by Las Vegas resident revelers for New Year's Eve. Each year since the advent of the Fremont Street Experience, the celebrations have become more elaborate with live music and other entertainment; food and beverages; a countdown to midnight; fireworks; and dancing in the streets. Of course, there are paper hats, noisemakers, and serpentines, too. But, unlike most Fremont Street happenings on all other days of the year, the New Year's Eve festivities are not free.

Vegas Vic Sign

Fifty feet (16 m) tall, Vegas Vic is a survivor from the early casino days. In bygone days not only did he smoke and wave but he also talked, saying "Howdy pardner, welcome to Las Vegas." Now, Vic's voice box works only sometimes, but he still provides the backdrop for thousands of visitors' photographs each year. ◈ *25 Fremont Street • Map K4*

Mormon Fort

9 World's Largest Slot Machine, Four Queens

According to the Guinness World of Records Museum, the enormous eight-reel contraption within the Four Queens Hotel-Casino is the largest slot machine in the world. Up to six players at a time insert from one- to three-dollar tokens into the slot of the 9-ft (3-m) tall and 18-ft (6-m) wide machine; an employee pulls the giant-size handle; and everyone watching holds their breath. Winning combinations are posted on the machine. Should you be tempted to try, bear in mind that the more reels a machine has, the more difficult it is to hit winning combinations. ✪ *202 E. Fremont St. • Map K4*

10 Jackie Gaughan's Plaza Hotel-Casino Railroad Station

From Main Street, Jackie Gaughan's may look like just another casino, but if you walk on through you will find railroad tracks on the back side. The railroad station justifiably claims to be the only one in the world that is inside a casino, which was built around the existing Union Pacific Railroad depot in the 1970s. A map of the railroad's West Coast–Eastern Utah route is illustrated with an old-fashioned iron horse and a futuristic bullet train. Note that Main Street Station is further north. ✪ *1 Fremont St at Main Street • Map J4*

Downtown After Dark

Late Afternoon

Begin your excursion in the mid- to late afternoon, with a flying visit to the **Mormon Fort** (see p79). Allow more time if you are a history buff.

Next, head south to browse the **Bonanza Gift Shop**. Take a look around **Pawn Shop Plaza** while it is still light, then, as dusk deepens and the lights of Fremont Street begin to beguile, start exploring the **Glitter Gulch** nightlife (p79).

Try dining at one of the top restaurants in downtown, such as Vic and Anthony's at the Golden Nugget Casino (129 Fremont St), with its black-and-white decor, or the romantic Hugo's Cellar at Four Queens (202 Fremont St).

Nighttime

After dinner, stroll along Fremont Street's pedestrian promenade, stopping in at the shops that catch your eye and the vendors' carts that capture your fancy. If gaming's your pleasure, step inside the El Cortez Hotel's casino (600 Fremont Street).

Check out the train station at the **Plaza**, then wander down to Main Street Station. Pick up a brochure here with a map and list of treasures – including street lamps from Brussels and a portion of the Berlin wall – that are incorporated into the building's decor.

Back at **Fremont Street Experience** (p79), watch a light and sound show, then head to **Stratosphere** (p79) to top off the night with a stunning view of the city.

Left **Golden Gate shrimp cocktail** Right **Sport Club Hall of Fame**

🔟 Low-Cost Food & Entertainment

1 Fremont Street Experience

Seven light and sound shows, *Queen Tribute*, *Aria*, *Lucky Vegas*, *Above & Beyond*, *Fahrenheit*, *Area 51*, and *Ophelia's Dream* appear overhead on the hour until midnight in the arcade *(see p79)*. There are street performers and live music on mobile stages, too. ◎ *Map K4*

2 In-N-Out Burger

The nation's oldest drive-through burger chain is just the place for people who are hungry but don't have time to stop. ◎ *4888 Dean Martin Dr • Map R1*

3 Golden Gate Shrimp Cocktails

For years, fresh shrimp cocktails have been the loss leader at the Golden Gate – they have sold more than 35 million. The cost: 99 cents. ◎ *1 Fremont Street • Map K4*

4 Sport Club Hall of Fame

This free hotel-lobby museum includes bats swung by top baseball players and aerial views of major stadiums. ◎ *Las Vegas Club, 18 Fremont Street • Map K4*

5 Sam Boyd's Margaritas

Connoisseurs swear that the 99-cent margaritas, with just the right amount of salt rimming the chilled glass, are as good as any you can find elsewhere at many times the price. ◎ *Sam Boyd's Fremont Hotel & Casino, 200 Fremont Street • Map K4*

6 Lucky 7's Buffet

A short stroll from the Fremont Street Experience *(see p79)*, the Plaza's in-house buffet includes a prime rib carving station and is $7.77 per person all day. ◎ *Plaza Las Vegas Hotel & Casino, 1 Main St S. • Map K4*

7 Sourdough Cafe

A relic of a bygone era, this East Las Vegas casino's no-frills cafeteria serves eggs with ham or steak for $3.29, 24 hours a day. ◎ *Arizona Charlie's Boulder Casino, 4575 Boulder Hwy • Map E4*

8 Golden Gate Hot Dogs

All-beef frankfurters piled high with sauerkraut are served from a vendor cart in the casino's sports book (the lounge where people bet on sporting events). The hot dogs cost 75 cents.

9 Penny Video Poker Machines

The penny slot machines of the early casinos have disappeared from all but a few places such as the Four Queens – you're more likely to spend 45 or even 90 cents with every pull. ◎ *Four Queens Hotel and Casino, 202 E. Fremont St • Map K4*

10 Monorails

There are three monorails that navigate the Strip: Sahara–MGM Grand (single ride $5, one-day pass $15); TI–Mirage (free); and Excalibur–Mandalay Bay (free).

For more information on the monorails tel: 702 699 8299 or visit www.lvmonorail.com

Left **Vendor cart** Center **Bonanza Gift Shop** Right **Ray's Beaver Bag sign**

Places to Shop

1 Gambler's Book Shop

Come here for volumes on slot machines, horse racing, card games, casino management, probability, and playing strategies. ✆ 630 S. 11th Street • Map K5

2 Ray's Beaver Bag

Items recollect pioneer life in America, such as capes made of Hudson Bay blankets (called capotes), beaver skin bags, red flannel underwear, and black powder muskets. ✆ 2619 Ashby Ave • Map K4

3 The Attic

This claims to be the largest vintage clothing store in the world, where the young and hip make everything new again. Even the building has a distinctly retro feel. *(See also p91.)* ✆ 1018 S. Main Street • Map C3

4 Gambler's General Store

An intriguing place even for non-gamblers, this huge store is devoted to gaming paraphernalia. There are dice tables, roulette wheels, antique slot machines, and the "shoes" from which cards are dealt in blackjack. ✆ 800 S. Main Street • Map K4

5 Bonanza Gift Shop

The list of merchandise at this enormous store is as long as the souvenir manufacturers' imaginations. Anything at all that can be marketed as a memento of a visit to Las Vegas will be found here. *(See also p80.)*

6 Las Vegas Premium Outlets

Close to downtown, this outlet park has 120 stores selling a range of clothing, household goods, gifts, jewelry, and food. Stores include Banana Republic, Armani Exchange, and Coach. ✆ 875 S. Grand Central Parkway • Map J3

7 Red Rooster Antique Mall

Located in the city's Arts District, this co-operative's emphasis is on 20th-century collectibles, such as 1950s furniture, vintage clothing, and gaming paraphernalia. There are lots of dealers all with their own stalls (and their own opening times). ✆ 1109 Western Ave • Map L3

8 Beef Jerky Store

Smoked salmon, roasted soybeans, dried plums, glazed apricots, and *biscotti* are sold alongside dozens of varieties of jerky (sun-dried meat). ✆ 112 N. 3rd Street • Map J4

9 El Portal Southwest

Native Americans produce and sell goods within the historic El Portal movie theater building. ✆ 310 Fremont St • Map K4

10 Vendors' Carts

Carts placed at intervals down the center of the Fremont Street mall offer sunglasses, wind chimes, stuffed toys, baseball caps, and mini-cars in various makes and models. ✆ Map K4

Left **Las Vegas Speedway** Center **Chinatown Plaza** Right **Henderson Farmers Market**

Beyond the Neon

LOOK BEYOND THE NEON *and you will find that Las Vegas is, like the god Janus, a two-faced town. One is about make-up and make-believe; the other is like that of other American towns, with more than 500 churches, first-rate community centers, parks, and playgrounds. Las Vegas is a city where significant research is undertaken at medical centers, and where cultural performances take place almost every night. It is also a growing city with many ethnic neighborhoods.*

Left **Botanical gardens, UNLV** Right **UNLV campus**

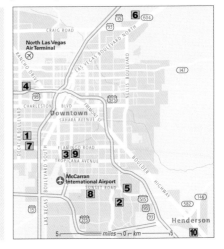

Chinatown Plaza

With pagoda-style roofs, a traditional Chinese entrance gate, and a statue of the mythical monk Tripitaka, with his companions – a pig, a soldier, and a monkey – Chinatown Plaza offers a delightful blend of East and West. Stores specialize in both American and Eastern necessities and Asian luxuries. Chinese music wafts through the covered walkways (a misting system keeps shoppers cool in summer). Good stops include Valley Oriental Arts and Crafts and Chinatown Florist. Not surprisingly, the restaurants are the best in town for Asian cuisine. *4215 Spring Mountain Rd • Map B4*

Foxridge Park

One of the most pleasant parks in the Las Vegas area, Foxridge Park has been the setting every September since 1994 for the "Shakespeare in the Park" festival. Each year a different work by Shakespeare is presented to the crowds. The Green Show preceding each performance features mimes, jugglers, and madrigal singers. All shows are free. *Valle Verde Drive just north of Warm Springs Rd, Henderson • Map E6*

UNLV Campus

City residents' favorite areas for taking a walk include the campus of the University of Nevada Las Vegas, which was established in 1957. The university may not have any remarkable buildings, but there are shade trees, and in early evening the paths are blissfully uncrowded. Be sure not to miss the desert garden, which is lovely. *4504 S. Maryland Parkway • Map Q4*

Nevada State Museum and Historical Society

The Nevada State Museum system is one of the best in the United States, and this Las Vegas branch is well deserving of a visit. The emphasis is on the anthropology and natural history of southern Nevada, with dioramas containing stuffed examples of regional wildlife such as a mountain lion a young bighorn sheep, a cougar, a bobcat, and a roadrunner On a totally different subject, head for the excellent Cowboy Up! exhibition, which charts more than 100 years of rodeo history. Temporary displays include items such as Indian baskets, fiber arts, and saddle blankets. *(See also p45)*

Chinatown Plaza

Casinos Beyond the Neon

Although for the past 30 years Las Vegas has been a sprawling city with shopping centers and clusters of businesses in the various neighborhoods, almost all of the hotel/casinos were concentrated in two areas – downtown and along the Strip. In the 1980s, when the city's population began its explosive growth, a number of neighborhood hotel/casinos were built. Visitors who venture beyond the neon for gaming may be pleasantly surprised to find a friendly atmosphere and lovely surroundings *(see p88)*.

Ethel M. Chocolate Factory

Take a free tour to view the glass-enclosed, spotless, white kitchens where the diligent candymakers concoct their sweet creations. Find out what the large stainless steel machines do, and admire the finished confections wrapped in their foil of emerald, ruby, sapphire, and other jewel colors. Every tour participant receives a free chocolate at the end of the tour. Outside the factory is a lovely cactus garden, with plants clearly identified. ❂ *2 Cactus Garden Drive, Henderson • Map E5 • Open 8:30am–6pm daily • Free*

Ethel M. Chocolate Factory

Sunset Park

Las Vegas Speedway and Carroll Shelby Museum

Completed in 1996, the 142,000-seat Las Vegas Speedway was the first new super-speedway to be built in the southwest USA in more than two decades. The 1,600-acre facility has 14 different race tracks, food courts, three levels of open-air grandstand viewing, VIP party rooms, and 102 luxury skybox suites. Important races staged here include the Sam's Town 300. A museum in the grounds is devoted to the famous automotive designer and former racing driver Carroll Shelby and his beautiful cars. ❂ *6755 Speedway Blvd • 702 644 4444 • Map E1 • Call for museum opening times and tours*

Masquerade Village Show in the Sky

The complex is designed to resemble an idyllic fishing village in northern Italy, complete with window boxes and balconies. The "Show in the Sky" consists of four lavish floats that travel on a track suspended above the village perimeter. Costumed performers toss beads and trinkets to the audience below. ❂ *Rio Suite Hotel, 3700 W. Flamingo Rd; • Map C4 • 702 252 7777 • Hourly shows 3–9:30pm • Admission charge to ride*

Sunset Park

Undeniably the city's most popular park, Sunset offers

basketball, tennis, and jogging *(see p61)*; a place to fly kites and sail boats; some of the best picnic spots in town; and a swimming pool. There's a dog run, too. ◈ *2601 E. Sunset Rd • Map D5*

9 Marjorie Barrick Museum of Natural History

The museum centers around desert mammals, reptiles, and insects native to the southwest. It also contains exhibits on the area's anthropology, archeology, and early-day architecture. ◈ *UNLV campus • Map Q4 • 702 895 3381 • Open 8am–4:45pm Mon–Fri, 10am–2pm Sat • Free (contributions suggested)*

10 Henderson Farmers Market

The market had its beginnings in 1999 and gets bigger each season. Farmers drive from the California valleys to sell their produce year-round; in the summer season, they're joined by Nevada growers. No matter the season, artisans are on hand, selling everything from hand-painted china and rag dolls to house plants and chess sets. ◈ *Civic Center Plaza, 240 Water St, Henderson • Map G6 • 702 565 2181 • Open 11am–6pm Thu*

Masquerade Village in the Sky

Two Excursions Beyond the Neon

Morning

🕐 Begin with an early morning stroll around the UNLV campus, stopping at the **Marjorie Barrick Museum of Natural History.**

Drive through the Green Valley area to **Foxridge Park** *(see p85)* where if children are in your party, the play equipment will be the main attraction. Then it's on to the **Ethel M. Chocolate Factory** for the free tour and walk around the cactus garden.

On the way back to your hotel, lunch at one of the terrace tables around the **interactive fountains at Green Valley Center** *(see p66)*. You'll have the afternoon free, but if it's Friday, don't miss the **Henderson Farmers Market**. Or, if traffic is not too heavy, you can take a second excursion.

Afternoon

Begin at the **Nevada State Museum and Historical Society** *(see p85)*. Motorracing fans should then make their next stop the **Las Vegas Speedway**.

🕐 Finish up at **Chinatown Plaza** *(see p85)*, where the herbalist health-food shop is a repository for remedies such as dried sea horses (good for the kidneys)

After an hour or two shopping, head up to the second floor of the Plaza, where you have a choice of different Asian restaurants for dining. Among them are Pho Vietnam Restaurant, Kapit Bahay Filipino Fast Food, Sam Woo BBQ, and Mother's Grill.

Left **J. W. Marriott Las Vegas** Center **Sunset Station** Right **Texas Station**

TOP 10 Casinos

1 Rio
The Rio has more video poker machines than most, and a friendly feeling associated with casinos that rely on local trade for repeat business. *(See also p36.)* ✆ *3700 W. Flamingo Rd • Map C4 • 702 252 7777*

2 J. W. Marriott Las Vegas
A great place during daytime for people who want to gamble in a quiet, relaxing, upscale atmosphere. *(See also p36.)* ✆ *221 N. Rampart Blvd • Map A3 • 702 869 7777*

3 Santa Fe Station
A mid-size gambling floor (2,900 slots), the Santa Fe is patronized primarily by locals and is one of the more pleasant casinos beyond the neon *(See also p36.)* ✆ *4949 N. Rancho Drive • Map A1 • 702 658 4900*

4 Loews Lake Las Vegas
The hands-down winner for surroundings, with sweeping views of the lake and mountains. *(See also p37.)* ✆ *101 Monte Lago Blvd, Henderson • Map H4 • 702 567 1234*

5 Fiesta Rancho
From cocktail waitresses in jewel-toned satin outfits to the gaily patterned carpets on the floor, the casino evokes party time. *(See also p37.)* ✆ *2400 N. Rancho Drive • Map B2 • 702 631 7000*

6 Texas Station
The theme is of a 19th-century town in the Lone Star state of Texas, with wagon wheels and gunpowder barrels. ✆ *2101 N. Rancho Drive • Map B2 • 702 631 1000*

7 Sunset Station
Mediterranean-themed casino with wrought-iron balconies. Natural light makes it more pleasant than most. ✆ *1301 W. Sunset Rd, Henderson • Map F6 • 702 547 7777*

8 Sam's Town
One of the largest non-Strip casinos with 3,300 slots, video poker, and keno machines. ✆ *5111 Boulder Hwy, Las Vegas • Map E4 • 702 456 7777*

9 The Orleans
There's a feeling of Mardi Gras in the casino, which is patterned after New Orleans' Vieux Carré. ✆ *4500 W. Tropicana Ave • Map B4 • 702 365 7111*

10 Arizona Charlie's
Dude-ranch touches include deer antler chandeliers. Pai gow poker and Royal Match 21 are included in the games. ✆ *740 S. Decatur Blvd • Map B3 • 702 258 5200*

Price Categories

For a standard, double room per night (with breakfast if included), taxes, and extra charges.

$	under $50
$$	$50–$100
$$$	$100–$150
$$$$	$150–$200
$$$$$	over $200

Left **Polo Towers** Right **Rio All-Suite Hotel**

🔟 Hotels and Motels

J. W. Marriott Las Vegas
Composed of two hotels, the Palms Tower Hotel and the Spa Tower Hotel, with great restaurants such as Gustave Mauler's Spiedini Ristorante. ✆ *221 N. Rampart Blvd • Map A3 • 702 869 7777 • $$$$*

Loews Lake Las Vegas
The 496 guest rooms offer great views and all kinds of upscale facilities to round out the charms of this golfers' paradise. ✆ *101 Monte Lago Blvd, Henderson • Map H4 • 702 567 1234 • $$$$$*

Polo Towers
Condominium offering nightly rentals when the units are not occupied by time-share members. Great for families. ✆ *3745 Las Vegas Blvd S. • Map C4 • 702 261 1000 • $$$*

Rio All-Suite Hotel
Perfect for visitors who want the total resort experience without the congestion of the Strip. *(See also p33.)* ✆ *3700 W. Flamingo Ave • Map C4 • 888 396 2483 • $$$*

Palms Hotel & Casino
With only 425 rooms, Palms is small by Las Vegas standards. Its nightclub, Rain, attracts a younger crowd. ✆ *4321 W. Flamingo Rd • Map C4 • 702 942 7777 • $$$*

Courtyard by Marriott
Popular with trade show attendees. Dining away from the crowds is a real plus. ✆ *3275 Paradise Rd • Map C4 • 702 791 3600 • $$$$*

The Orleans
French Quarter-themed hotel, with green-shuttered windows and wrought-iron balconies. ✆ *4500 W. Tropicana Ave • Map B4 • 702 365 7111 • $$*

Sunset Station
Experience almost all the Las Vegas diversions in an away-from-the-Strip location: shopping at the Galleria *(see p52)*, golf, and casino action. ✆ *1301 W. Sunset Rd, Henderson • Map F6 • 702 547 7777 • $$$*

Ritz Carlton
This Mediterranean-style lakeside resort has 349 luxurious rooms with panoramic views of the mountains or lake. Excellent restaurant and spa. ✆ *1610 Lake Las Vegas Parkway, Henderson • Map H4 • 702 567 4700 • $$$$$*

Santa Fe Station
A hit with people who love vacations for its ice skating rink and 60-lane bowling alley. Golf packages are also available. ✆ *4949 N. Rancho Drive • Map A1 • 702 658 4900 • $$*

Note: All hotels listed accept credit cards, have air conditioning, and rooms with private bathrooms

Price Categories

For a three course meal for one with a half bottle of wine (or equivalent meal), taxes and extra charges.	**$** under $20
	$$ $20–$30
	$$$ $30–$45
	$$$$ $45–£60
	$$$$$ over $60

Left **Wienerschnitzel** Right **Big Mama's**

🔟 Family Restaurants

1 Fatburger
Big, handmade burgers, hearty fries, and a classic 1950s atmosphere make Fatburger a top Las Vegas hamburger destination. A rock 'n' roll jukebox adds a note of authenticity and old-fashioned charm to the decor. ◈ *4851 Charleston Blvd • Map C3 • 702 870 4933 • $*

2 Hard Rock Café
Huge three-decker bacon, lettuce, and tomato sandwiches, great hamburgers, and fresh apple cobbler. ◈ *4475 Paradise Rd • Map Q3 • 702 733 7625 • $$*

3 Original Pancake House
The portions are huge; the pancakes, divine. And so many varieties – blueberry, apple, plate-size German pancakes, or buttermilk hotcakes as small as silver dollars. ◈ *4833 W. Charleston Blvd • Map B3 • 702 259 7755 • $*

4 Omelet House
This low-key breakfast spot serves the under-10 crowd meals big enough to satisfy an adult. ◈ *2160 W. Charleston Blvd • Map L2 • 702 384 6868 • $*

5 Wienerschnitzel
Drive-thru hotdog stand, with both the traditional pickles-with-mustard dogs and variations. ◈ *4001 W. Sahara Ave (and other locations) • Map B3 • 702 362 0418 • $*

6 Romano's Macaroni Grill
Bruschetta with a selection of toppings, fried mozzarella cheese, Italian *panini* sandwiches, and mouth-watering pasta. ◈ *2400 W. Sahara • Map B3 • 702 248 9500 • $$*

7 Souper Salad
Soups, muffins, and salads that are a real bargain, especially on Sundays when children eat for under $1. ◈ *2051 N. Rainbow Blvd • Map A2 • 702 631 2604 • $*

8 Big Mama's Rib Shack & Soul Food
Creole and Cajun dishes such as jambalaya, creole gumbo, okra, fish cakes, and sweet potato pie. ◈ *2230 W. Bonanza Rd • Map D3 • 702 597 1616 • $*

9 Jamm's on Rainbow Blvd
The place for breakfast: scrumptious french toast and eggs fixed to your liking. ◈ *1029 S. Rainbow Blvd • Map A4 • 702 877 0749 • $$*

10 Buca di Beppo
There are family-style platters and hefty bottles of wine to be had at this authentic Italian dining experience. ◈ *412 East Flamingo Rd • Map Q3 • 702 866 2867 • $$*

For salad bars, buffets, and brunches **See pp48–9**

Left **Indoor Swap Meet** Center **The Attic Rag Co.** Right **Chinatown Plaza**

🔟 Shopping

1 Chinatown Plaza
A shopping center that serves the needs of the city's sizeable Asian community as well as Asian-American tourists and visitors from around the world. At festival times *(see p58)*, counters are piled high with moon cakes and treats linked to special days. *(See also p85.)*

2 The Attic Rag Co.
The largest vintage clothing store in the world, with 1940s pillbox hats and rhinestone jewelry, 1960s tuxedos, and 1950s-style hot pants and sequined eyeglasses. ⊗ *1018 S. Main St • Map K3 • www.atticvintage.com*

3 Sampler Shoppes Antiques & Collectibles Mall
Casino memorabilia and the largest array of antiques in Las Vegas. ⊗ *6115 W. Tropicana Ave • Map D4*

4 Las Vegas Outlet Center
A truly fabulous place for any shoppers in your party who may have "champagne" tastes but "house-wine" wallets. *(See also p53.)* ⊗ *7400 Las Vegas Blvd S. • Map C6*

5 Fantastic Indoor Swap Meet
The Swap Meet is the American equivalent of the European flea market: vintage kitchen appliances, tire chains, home-baked bread, mismatched chairs, etc. ⊗ *Decatur Blvd at W. Oakey • Map B3 • Open weekends*

6 Cost Plus World Market
Import bazaar with handsome tableware, furniture, foodstuffs, and art objects from all corners of the world. ⊗ *3840 S. Maryland Parkway • Map D4*

7 Shepler's
Nevada cowboys buy their bolo ties, boots, sheepskin jackets, big belt buckles, and cowboy hats here. ⊗ *3035 E. Tropicana Ave • Map D5*

8 Serge's Showgirl Wigs
The hairpieces are favored by top hairdressers for production shows and Hollywood films. ⊗ *953 East Sahara Ave • Map D3*

9 Bell, Book, & Candle
Talismans, crystal balls, tarot cards, and other soothsayers' tools. Witchcraft lessons, too. ⊗ *1725 E. Charleston Blvd • Map D3*

10 Thriller Clothing
Provocative swimwear, sexy shoes, and evening wear advertised as "tasteful and classy." ⊗ *855 E. Twain Ave • Map E4*

For more on shopping **See pp 52–5, 83 & 116**

Left **Hoover Dam** Center **Boulder City/Hoover Dam Museum** Right **Lake cruiser, Lake Mead**

Lake Mead, Hoover Dam, and Laughlin

THE HOOVER DAM, MOST ASSUREDLY, *changed the face of the American West*. Not only did it enable the production of vast amounts of electrical energy and establish a reliable water source, but it also eliminated flooding, to help agriculture in California's lower valleys. The project's commercial by-products in Nevada – Lake Mead, Boulder City, and the resort community of Laughlin – have infused billions of dollars into the state's economy and provided recreational opportunities for hundreds of millions of visitors.

Left **View from Hoover Dam Visitor Center** Right **Lake Mead**

🔟 Sights Around Lake Mead and Laughlin

1. Hoover Dam Tour
2. Boulder City Historic District
3. Boulder City/Hoover Dam Museum
4. Lake Mead National Recreation Area
5. Lake Mead Marinas and Beaches
6. Laughlin's Casino Row
7. Lake Mojave
8. Petroglyphs near Laughlin
9. Oatman, Arizona
10. Avi Resort and Casino

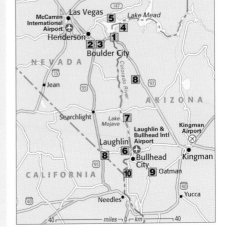

Hoover Dam Tour

Hoover Dam Tour

Self-guided tours lead to six points around the dam, where guides give short talks on the dam's history and construction. The Bureau of Reclamation opened an impressive $125 million visitor center and parking lot in 1995. The three-level, circular center includes a rooftop overlook, a rotating theater, and a gallery. Here you can learn the fascinating story of the settlement of the lower Colorado River valley and find out about the amazing technology involved in the production and distribution of hydroelectric power. *(See also p10.)* ✪ *Visitor Center, Hoover Dam • 702 294 3521 • Tour reservations 866 291 TOUR*

Boulder City Historic District

It's worth including Boulder City on a Hoover Dam trip to appreciate the scale of work involved – the city was built as a model community to house dam construction workers. The grandest buildings are the Bureau of Reclamation and the Bureau of Power and Light; the Municipal Building; and the Boulder Dam Hotel. Most of the construction, however, was focused on the two- and three-room houses for the workers. *(See also p11.)* ✪ *Information from Hoover Dam Museum • Hwy 93 at Lakeshore Rd • 702 294 1988*

Boulder City/ Hoover Dam Museum

Built in 1933, the Dutch Colonial-style Boulder Dam Hotel now houses the Boulder City/Hoover Dam Museum. Actor Boris Karloff and other Hollywood stars stayed in the hotel's glory days, and Crown Prince Olav and Princess Martha of Norway hosted a party here in 1939. The out-of-town hotel declined in the postwar rise of Las Vegas as a tourist mecca, but, since the mid-90s, a group of volunteers has set about rehabilitating it. The museum itself includes memorabilia from the 1930s. *(See also p11.)* ✪ *1305 Arizona St, Boulder City • 702 294 1988 • Open 10am–5pm Mon–Sat, noon–5pm Sun • Admission charge*

Lake Mead National Recreation Area

After the completion of the Hoover Dam in 1935, the waters of the Colorado River filled the deep canyons that once towered above the river to create a huge reservoir. This lake, with its 700 miles (1,120 km) of shoreline, is the centerpiece of Lake Mead National Recreation Area, a 1.5-million-acre (600,000-ha) tract of land. ✪ *Information from Alan Bible Visitor Center • Hwy 93 at Lakeshore Rd • 702 293 8990 • www.nps.gov/lame*

Boulder City Historic District

For more on the Hoover Dam **See pp10–11**

Around the Region – Lake Mead, Hoover Dam, and Laughlin

The Laughlin Story

Don Laughlin opened his four-unit motel and bar with about a dozen slot machines on the banks of the Colorado River in the same week in 1966 as the opulent Caesars Palace opened in Las Vegas. Laughlin town (named by the postmaster in 1977) is now Nevada's third busiest gambling destination – outranked only by Las Vegas and Reno.

Casino Row, Laughlin

may not be as dazzling as those along the Las Vegas Strip, but they offer extremely good value. Getting around is easier than in Las Vegas: a riverside promenade connects most of the casinos, or you can take a bus or shuttle boat. Tours of the Colorado are also available. ◈ 90 miles (145 km) S. of Las Vegas • www.enjoylaughlin.com

5 Lake Mead Marinas and Beaches

Along many miles of varied shoreline, Lake Mead's marinas and beaches range from delightful tiny coves to long stretches of sand. Popular beaches include Boulder Beach, Callville Bay, Echo Bay, and Overton Beach. These have recreational vehicle sites with full hookups, and supplies at nearby stores. Boxcar and Icebox coves are favorites with houseboaters. Callville Bay and Lake Mead marinas are close to Hoover Dam, while Temple Bar marina serves the lake's southeast reaches. ◈ Information from Alan Bible Visitor Center • 702 293 8990

6 Laughlin's Casino Row

The establishments lining Laughlin's South Casino Drive

7 Lake Mojave

The 67-mile (107-km) long lake extends from below Hoover Dam to 2 miles (3.5 km) north of Laughlin, and is only 4 miles (6.5 km) at its widest. A National Park Service Visitor Center at Katharine Landing, just north of Laughlin, offers free guided walks by park rangers. These lead through the desert to the petroglyphs at Grapevine Canyon. Houseboats, pontoon rentals, and fishing tackle are available at Katharine Landing and Cottonwood Cove. Record-size striped bass have been caught in Lake Mojave. ◈ Part of Lake Mead National Recreation Area • Admission fee to park • www.nps.gov/lame

8 Petroglyphs near Laughlin

Christmas Tree Pass and Grapevine Canyon, just west of Laughlin on Hwy 163, are the best places to see the fascinating petroglyphs incised into the cliffs of the canyons by the early Patayan group.

Echo Bay, Lake Mead

The line drawings and symbols may have served as the road maps of their day, directing hunters and fishermen. National Park Service personnel have located more than 150 Patayan camp sites between Davis Dam and Willow Beach, which is 10 miles (16 km) from the base of Hoover Dam. ◈ *Part of Lake Mead National Recreation Area • Admission fee to park • www.nps.gov/lame*

Petroglyph near Laughlin

Oatman, Arizona

A century ago, Oatman was a thriving gold mining center; today, visitors are taken back to the old days of the Wild West, with burros roaming the streets and staged gunfights in the middle of town. The Oatman Hotel was where honeymooners Clark Gable and Carole Lombard stayed in 1939. The town has been used as the location for a number of movies, including *How the West Was Won*.
◈ *General information 928 768 6222*

Avi Resort and Casino

In 1995, the Fort Mojave Indian tribe opened Nevada's first Native American-owned casino and the only Native American-owned gaming business in the USA operated under state regulations. "Avi" means money or loose change. The resort is located in an area that the tribe intends to develop as a planned community. *(See also p97.)*

Two Days at the Dam and Laughlin

Day One

Begin with early morning coffee at Railroad Pass Casino on Hwy 93, an old-timer among gambling dens. Afterward, continue on Hwy 93 to the historic **Boulder City** and **Hoover Dam** *(see p93)* for the amazing tour.

Go back along Hwy 93 to the junction with Hwy 95 and turn south toward Laughlin. Stop at the **Nugget** in Searchlight *(see p96)* for lunch and the chance to visit a typical small-town Nevada casino.

For a more picturesque route, turn off 95 and head east on the dirt road through Christmas Tree Pass. Spend the remainder of the day in **Laughlin**, perhaps hunting for bargains at the 50-store Horizon Discount Outlet.

Overnight at **Harrah's** *(see p97)* or another hotel along the river, and be sure to take an evening stroll along the promenade.

Day Two

Early next morning, golfers can tee off at the 18-hole Emerald River Golf Course. Alternatively, the River-view Golf Course is just across the river in Bullhead City, Arizona.

Later, head for **Oatman**, an old-time western town about a half-hour's drive southeast from Bullhead City. In the afternoon drive back north to **Lake Mojave**. Be sure to make time to see the mysterious **petro-glyphs** at Grapevine Canyon, off Hwy 163, before returning to your hotel in Laughlin.

Price Categories

For a three course meal for one with a half bottle of wine (or equivalent meal), taxes and extra charges.	
$	under $20
$$	$20–$30
$$$	$30–$45
$$$$	$45–60
$$$$$	over $60

Left **Bob's All Family Restaurant** Right **Sidewalk Café**

🔟 Places to Eat

1 Bradley's All Family Restaurant, Boulder City

The place to order home-made soup or chili and big slabs of pie. Decor is cozy, and the waitresses are small-town friendly. ✎ 761 Nevada Hwy • 702 294 2627 • $

2 Toto's Mexican Restaurant, Boulder City

Mexican standards – burritos, tacos, enchiladas – done with flair at this popular chain. ✎ 806 Buchanan Blvd • 702 293 1744 • $

3 Nugget Restaurant, Searchlight

Dominated by a mural of the *Searchlight*, an 1880s riverboat. The signature dish is a jumbo corn muffin with sausage, scrambled eggs, and gravy. ✎ 100 Highway 95 • 702 297 1201 • $

4 The Steakhouse, Laughlin

A perennial winner of *Casino Player Magazine's* best steak house award. It resembles a Victorian railroad parlor car with 19th-century-style gas lamps. ✎ Tropicana Express Hotel & Casino, 2121 S. Casino Drive • 702 298 4200 • $$

5 No Ka Oi Buffet, Laughlin

Laughlin's only 24-hour buffet provides an affordable, all-purpose dining option with colorful island decor. ✎ River Palms Resort Casino, 2700 S. Casino Drive • 800 835 7904 • $

6 Fresh Market Square, Harrah's, Laughlin

Salads of all sorts (pasta, potato, slaws, and gelatin), carved meats, fresh fruit, and a gala array of desserts. ✎ 2900 S. Casino Drive • 702 298 4600 • $$

7 Paradise Garden Buffet, Laughlin

Several sauté stations serve up fried catfish and Italian sausage. Crowd-pleasers include complimentary beer and wine and a make-your-own sundae bar. ✎ Aquarius Casino Resort, 1900 S. Casino Drive • 702 298 5111 • $

8 Granny's Champagne Brunch, Laughlin

This Sunday-only affair bans anyone under 21 or dressed in shorts, thongs, tank tops, or T-shirts. Blueberry blintzes, shrimp, escargots, caviar, crab legs, and wild rice often appear. ✎ Pioneer Hotel, 2200 S. Casino Drive • 702 298 2442 • $$

9 The Range, Laughlin

In addition to the traditional steaks and prime rib, you'll find the likes of scampi savoy and *crème brûlée* on the menu. ✎ Harrah's, 2900 S. Casino Drive • 702 298 6832 • $$$$

10 Sidewalk Café, Laughlin

Contemporary deli offering sandwiches, soups, salads, and pasta. ✎ 1650 S. Casino Drive • 702 298 2535 • $

Nugget, Searchlight

Recommend your favorite restaurant on traveldk.com

Price Categories

For a standard, double room per night (with breakfast if included), taxes, and extra charges.

$	under $50
$$	$50–$100
$$$	$100–$150
$$$$	$150–$200
$$$$$	over $200

Left **Harrah's, Laughlin** Right **Ramada Express Hotel and Casino**

🔟 Places to Stay and Casinos

1 Harrah's, Laughlin
Spanish-themed property with its own sand beach, a casino with windows looking out on the river, five restaurants, and a particularly pleasant ambience. ◈ 2900 S. Casino Drive • 800 447 8700 • www.harrahs.com • $

2 Golden Nugget Riverside, Laughlin
A tropical atrium with cascading waterfalls, palm trees, and 300 species of tropical plants sets this hotel apart. The casino, with its 24 Karat Slot Club, is more attractive than most. ◈ 2300 S. Casino Drive • 702 298 7111 • $

3 Don Laughlin's Riverside Resort, Laughlin
A total destination resort. Unusual features include two classic auto showrooms and an antique slot machine display. There's also an RV park with full hook-ups. ◈ 1650 S. Casino Drive • 702 298 2535 • $

4 Aquarius Casino Resort, Laughlin
The hotel features a large pool deck overlooking the river and Arizona hills, three lighted tennis courts, a wedding chapel, and Laughlin's largest tour boat, the Celebration. ◈ 1900 S. Casino Drive • 702 298 5111 • $

5 Tropicana Express Hotel and Casino, Laughlin
Advertised as "the premier destination for mature travelers." There's a Sunday flag-raising ceremony, a free multimedia show called On the Wings of Eagles, and a 1940s Museum of Memories. ◈ 2121 S. Casino Drive • 702 298 4200 • www.tropicanax.com • $

6 Avi Resort and Casino, near Laughlin
Native American-owned resort (see p95) with a large, sandy, riverside beach, video arcade, swimming pool, live entertainment, and 29 spa suites. ◈ Aha Macav Parkway • 702 535 5555 • $

7 Best Western Lighthouse Inn and Resort, Lake Mead
A 70-room motor hotel with views of Lake Mead. ◈ 110 Ville Drive • 702 293 6444 • $$

8 El Rancho Boulder Motel, Boulder City
Spanish-style motel on the main street. Some rooms have kitchens. ◈ 725 Nevada Hwy • 702 293 1085 • elranchobm@aol.com • $$

9 Overton Arm Campgrounds, Lake Mead
The campground offers showers, restrooms, and fuel. Reservations are not accepted. ◈ Close to the tip of the lake's northern arm • $

10 Seven Crown Resorts, Lake Mead
Houseboats in various sizes and with excellent facilities can be rented here. All houseboaters have to bring on deck are food and clothing. ◈ Highway 167, Echo Bay • 800 752 9669 • $$$$$

Left **Petroglyphs, Valley of Fire** Center **Death Valley** Right **Scotty's Castle, Death Valley**

Parks and Preserves

LESS THAN AN HOUR *from the man-made extravaganzas and simulations of the Strip are natural wonders so dramatic and thrilling that humans could not begin to replicate them. Many of these wonders are geological.* The closest is Red Rock Canyon (see pp24–5). Also nearby are Zion National Park, with its fantastic rock formations, and Death Valley – the hottest place in North America – whose floor lies 282 ft (85 m) below sea level, making it the lowest elevation in the western hemisphere. Most famous is undoubtedly Grand Canyon, whose dimensions are breathtaking. Each region has its distinct flora and fauna, with some species found nowhere else on Earth.

🔟 Sights of the Parks and Preserves

1. Petroglyph Canyon, Valley of Fire
2. Lost City Museum of Archeology, Overton
3. Kolob Reservoir Road, Zion National Park
4. Zion Canyon
5. Bright Angel Point, North Rim, Grand Canyon
6. Yavapai Observation Station, Grand Canyon
7. Watch Tower, Grand Canyon
8. Scotty's Castle, Death Valley
9. Aguereberry Point, Death Valley
10. Dante's View, Death Valley

Zion Lodge, Zion Canyon

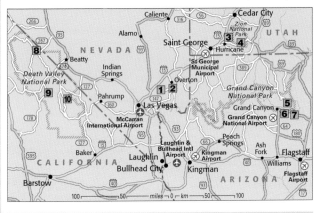

For more on the Grand Canyon See pp16–19

Left **Petroglyph Canyon** Right **Canyon Lodge, North Rim, Grand Canyon**

1 Petroglyph Canyon, Valley of Fire

Petroglyph Canyon is the Valley of Fire's most popular attraction, carrying as it does the park's largest concentration of petroglyphs – primarily symbols incised by prehistoric Native Americans from the Lost City (see below). The purpose of the petroglyphs is unclear: some may have been no more than the road signs of their day, while others might have had a religious or mystical significance. Trail markers point out interesting sites along the way. ⊗ Map U2 • 702 397 2088 • Admission charge for park

2 Lost City Museum of Archeology, Overton

Artifacts salvaged from Pueblo Grande de Nevada – now known as the Lost City – before it was inundated by Lake Mead are displayed at this pueblo-style museum. Exhibits include a reconstruction of the village, hunting weapons, and pottery. ⊗ 721 S. Moapa Valley Blvd, Overton • Map U2 • 702 397 2193 • Open 8:30am–4:30pm daily • admission charge

3 Kolob Reservoir Road, Zion National Park

Also called Kolob Terrace Road, this makes for a great scenic drive, taking in the multicolored Moenkopi Formation rocks, North Creek, Tabernacle Dome (a mass of red rock), cinder cones, canyons, valleys, and forests. ⊗ Map U1 • Information from Zion Canyon Visitor Center, Hwy 9, nr Springdale • 435 772 3256

4 Zion Canyon

This makes for another splendid scenic drive, ending at the Temple of Sinawava. Of special interest is a mass of debris caused by a landslide 4,000 years ago. If you can stay, head for Zion Lodge (see also p107), and, if you have no air-conditioning, gaze longingly at the shady groves of cottonwood, velvet ash, and box elder. Near the end of the drive is a turning that affords excellent views of the Great White Throne. ⊗ Map V1 • Information from Zion Canyon Visitor Center, Hwy 9, nr Springdale • 435 772 3256 • www.zionpark.com

5 Bright Angel Point, North Rim, Grand Canyon

The North Rim of Grand Canyon may be more remote than the South Rim, but it is worth the effort. From Bright Angel Point (situated on an ancient trail) are spectacular canyon views. ⊗ Map V2 • North Rim Visitor Center, Bright Angel Peninsula • Open May–Oct

View from the North Rim

Following pages **Death Valley**

Left **Hopi House by Mary Colter, Grand Canyon** Right **Road to Mount Zion**

6 Yavapai Observation Station, South Rim, Grand Canyon

For a visual introduction to Grand Canyon geology, you can scarcely beat the view from Yavapai Observation Station. Look down to the canyon floor for views of the Phantom Ranch lodge and the Colorado River. The river flows along the bottom of the canyon, no less than 5,000 ft (1,500 m) below the rim. From this great height it doesn't look very threatening, even with binoculars, but from the canyon floor it's a wildly impressive sight. ◔ *5 miles (8 km) N of south entrance • Map V2 • Open 8am–8pm*

7 The Watchtower, Desert View, Grand Canyon

A fanciful recreation of an Ancestral Pueblo, this landmark structure was designed by regional architect Mary Colter in 1932. The upper floor of the stone-built tower is decorated with Hopi murals. A gift store and refreshments are available. Other Colter designs in the area include Hopi House, Hermit's Rest, the Lookout Studio, and the cabins at Phantom Ranch lodge. ◔ *On Hwy 64 at Desert View • Map V2 • General infomation www.nps.gov/deva • Free*

Ancient Rocks

The Grand Canyon reveals more of the earth's geological history than anywhere else on the planet (some of its rocks may be 1.7 billion years old). The mesas and cliffs of Zion National Park, too, were laid down and sculpted by the elements over millions of years. The youngster, Death Valley, has become visible only in relatively recent times: the lake that once filled it dried up a mere 10,000 years ago.

8 Scotty's Castle, Death Valley

Less of a castle than a Mediterranean-style mansion, the main man-made visitor attraction at Death Valley was built in the 1920s by the Chicago insurance magnate Albert Johnson. But Wild West show cowboy and conman Walter Scott had a habit of bragging that the spread was his, and it came to be called Scotty's Castle after him. A nice twist to the tale is that, in his

Dante's View, Death Valley

Kolob Reservoir Road

last years, Scott was befriended by Johnson and spent his last years at the coveted castle. Tours of the interior are available year round: fine craftsmanship is evident in the intricate wood carvings, wrought iron, and ornate tiling. It is possible to take a self-guided tour of the grounds. *Hwy 267, at N. end of Death Valley • Map S1 • 760 786 2392 • Grounds 9am–5pm daily, guided tours hourly • Admission fee*

9 Aguereberry Point, Death Valley

High in the Panamint Mountains, the point offers panoramic views across most of Death Valley, taking in Furnace Creek, the snow-capped Sierra Nevada, Devil's Golf Course, and other landmarks. The point is accessible by mountain bike, but you'll need excellent bike-handling skills to make the climb; there is a 13-mile (21-km) loop ride for those who want to try it. *Map S2 • Information from Furnace Creek Visitor Center • 760 786 2331 • Open 8am–5pm*

10 Dante's View, Death Valley

On the crest of the Black Mountains, this is one of the most spectacular overlooks in Death Valley. It is approximately 5,475 ft (1,668 m) above the Badwater salt flats – the lowest point in Death Valley – and is a wonderful place for watching sunrise. The name was inspired by Dante's Inferno. *Dante's View Rd, 25 miles (40 km) S. of Furnace Creek • Map S2*

Three Trips from Vegas

Although it is possible to visit Zion, Grand Canyon, and Death Valley in one trip, it makes more sense geographically to return to Las Vegas in between each place, making three separate excursions.

The Road to Zion

For an overnight trip to remember, drive east on Highway 15 to the Valley of Fire turning. Spend an hour or two on the park's scenic drive, hiking through **Petroglyph Canyon** *(See p99)* to Mouse's Tank and visiting the **Lost City Museum of Archeology** *(See p99)*. Then, back on Highway 15, proceed to Mesquite for lunch, making sure you are within reach of one of Zion's many viewpoints by sunset: you will be richly rewarded. Overnight in the park or at Springdale.

Grand Canyon

Take Highway 93 to Kingman, then Highways 40 and 64 to the national park. It is possible to view much of the canyon's grandeur by driving along the rim routes, but the total canyon experience involves hiking or riding to the valley floor, spending the night, and perhaps river-rafting. For insights into Native American culture, visit one of the reservations along the rim.

Death Valley

Starting out from Las Vegas again, head north-west on Highway 95 to Beatty, turning off on Highway 374. You can see the major sights easily in a day and a half, but if you wish to hike or golf, you'll want to allocate more time to the trip.

For more information on touring the region **See p109**

Left **Pinon trees** Center Left **Iguana** Center right **Sagebrush** Right **Desert tortoise**

※10 Local Flora and Fauna

1 Pine Forests
Dense forests of scrubby piñon pine, stunted by poor, dry soil, grow 6,500 ft (2,000 m) above sea level in Grand Canyon (the canyon's highest elevation is 9,000 ft, or 2,750 m). Once every seven years they produce bumper crops of edible nuts.

2 Wildflowers
Grand Canyon wildflowers include asters, sunflowers, globemallow, and Indian paintbrush. At Zion, look out for columbine, penstemon, Indian paint-brush, and many varieties of sunflowers. Death Valley has fewer species, but Panamint daisies grow in profusion.

Golden Eagle

3 Sagebrush
The Nevada state flower is found up to 10,000 ft (3,000 m) above sea level and grows as tall as seven feet (2 m). The dense clusters of tiny yellow or cream flowers bloom in late summer.

4 Birds of Prey
Red-tailed hawks are the most common predatory birds in all three parks, but at the Grand Canyon look out for the king of the skies, the golden eagle.

5 Tortoises
Two isolated populations of desert tortoise, the Mojave and the Sonoran, are found respect-ively in southern Utah and in the Grand Canyon, Death Valley, and other parts of the southwest.

6 Lizards
In Zion eastern fence lizards are among 13 local species, while chuckwallas, short-horned, and collared lizards all inhabit the Grand Canyon. Most common in Death Valley is the banded lizard.

7 Mountain Lions
These shy creatures roam the Grand Canyon, Zion, and the mountains around Death Valley, helping to control the small mammal populations.

8 Deer
The unmistakable stiff-legged jump and large ears of the mule deer distinguish it through your binoculars from its graceful relative, the white-tail deer.

9 Snakes
Most species in the parks are harmless, but give rattlesnakes and sidewinders a wide berth.

10 Bears
Black bears are occasionally seen on the higher plateaus at Zion, but both they and grizzlies have long since disappeared from the Grand Canyon area, and no bears are known to live in the mountains surrounding Death Valley.

For desert precautions **See p133**

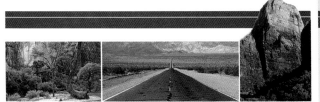

Left **Temple of Sinawava** Center **Panamint Mountains** Right **Great White Throne**

⁝10 Natural Formations

1 Atlatl Rock, Valley of Fire
The most famous petroglyph here depicts an *atlatl*, a notched stick used to add speed and distance to a thrown spear. ✎ *Map U2*

2 Elephant Rock, Valley of Fire
Accessible via a short trail from the eastern entrance, this strange sandstone formation resembles an elephant's head – albeit with an oversize trunk. ✎ *Map U2*

3 Temple of Sinawava, Zion National Park
The so-called temple is, in fact, an awe-inspiring mass of red rock. The religious name echoes many others in the park. ✎ *Map V1*

4 Great White Throne, Zion National Park
The sheer face of the Great White Throne, familiar to climbers worldwide, rises a staggering 2,200 ft (670 m) from the canyon floor, making it one of the world's tallest monoliths. ✎ *Map V1*

5 Kolob Arch, Zion National Park
Kolob Arch is too inaccessible to permit accurate measurements of its bulk, but it is thought to be as much as 230 ft high and 310 ft wide (70 m x 95 m). ✎ *Map V1*

6 Marble Canyon, Grand Canyon
The confluence of the Little Colorado and Colorado Rivers has carved out the great Marble Canyon (which is also a great place for trout fishing). ✎ *Map V2*

7 Inner Gorge, Grand Canyon
Sheer granite cliffs drop 1,000 feet (300 m) to the canyon floor to form this vertiginous gorge. Two nerve-testing suspension bridges make the crossing near Phantom Ranch. ✎ *Map V2*

8 San Francisco Mountains, Grand Canyon
Named the "Kingdom of St. Francis" by explorer Marcos de Nizo, the range rises to an impressive 12,655 ft (3,857 m). ✎ *Map V2*

9 Funeral Mountains, Death Valley
A geological fault line was responsible for tilting these spectacular mountains on their sides. ✎ *Map S1*

10 Panamint Mountains, Death Valley
The Panamints are honorary park members, lying as they do just outside it. Head for Agavereberry Point for amazing views of the Funeral Mountains and the Sierra Nevada beyond. ✎ *Map S2*

Funeral Mountains

For more on the Grand Canyon **See pp16–19**

Price Categories

For a three course meal for one with a half bottle of wine (or equivalent meal), taxes and extra charges.	**$** under $20
	$$ $20–$30
	$$$ $30–$45
	$$$$ $45– 60
	$$$$$ over $60

Left **Thunderbird, Zion** Right **Flanigan's Café, Zion**

🔟 Places to Eat

1 El Tovar Dining Room, Grand Canyon

The room is built of pine logs and stone and features fine china, crystal, and linen-covered tables. Fresh seafood is flown in daily, and the veal dishes are excellent. ◈ *El Tovar Hotel, South Rim • Map V2 • 928 638 2526 • $$$$*

2 Coronado Room, Grand Canyon

Prime rib, chicken marsala, and stuffed trout are favorites at this Spanish-style eatery.
◈ *Best Western Squire Inn, Tusayan • Map V2 • 928 638 2681 • $$$*

El Tovar Dining Room

3 Bright Angel Lodge Restaurant, Grand Canyon

Hearty Southwest American fare. ◈ *Bright Angel Lodge • Map V2 • 928 638 2526 • $$*

4 Arizona Steak House, Grand Canyon

A Southwest decor in muted pastels is the setting for the all-American favorite of big steaks, baked potatoes, and crisp salads. ◈ *Bright Angel Lodge • Map V2 • 928 638 2526 • $$$*

5 Maswik Lodge Cafeteria, Grand Canyon

Wholesome food at reasonable prices. For a pre- or post-meal drink, the lodge includes a sports bar with wide-screen TV. ◈ *Map V2 • Maswik Lodge • 303 297 2757 • $$*

6 Flanigan's Café, Zion

Among the house specialties are salads, pasta, red trout, chicken, Utah lamb, and Black Angus beef. ◈ *Springdale • Map U1 • 435 772 3244 • Open for dinner only • $$$*

7 Kolob Canyon Picnic Area, Zion

Buy picnic provisions at Oscar's Deli and a bumbleberry pie at the Bumbleberry Restaurant in Springdale for an al fresco meal in grander surroundings than any restaurant. ◈ *Map U1 • $$*

8 Thunderbird Resort Dining Room, Zion

American fare in a family dining room, where the pies, breads, and sweet rolls are homemade. ◈ *Mt Carmel Jtn • Map U1 • 435 648 2203 • $$*

9 The Inn Dining Room, Death Valley

Elegant dining room with lace tablecloths, firelight flickering on the adobe walls, and views of the Panamint Mountains. Continental fare is served in a six-course, prix fixe menu (try braised lamb shanks as your entrée). ◈ *Furnace Creek Inn • Map S1 • 760 786 2361 • $$$$$*

10 Stovepipe Wells Village, Death Valley

The Toll Road Restaurant offers typical fare, such as an all-you-can-eat buffet in summer. ◈ *Stovepipe Wells • Map S2 • 760 786 2387 • $$*

Recommend your favorite restaurant on traveldk.com

Around the Region – Parks and Preserves

Price Categories

For a standard, double room per night (with breakfast if included), taxes, and extra charges.

$	under $50
$$	$50–$100
$$$	$100–$150
$$$$	$150–$200
$$$$$	over $200

Left **Best Western Zion Park Inn** Right **Furnace Creek Inn**

🔟 Places to Stay

Best Western Squire Inn, Grand Canyon

The 250-room inn has its own tennis court, heated pool, sauna, billiards, video games, beauty salon, and bowling alley. ⚲ *Tusayan • Map V2 • 928 638 2681 • $$$*

El Tovar Hotel, Grand Canyon

Historic hotel built by pioneer resort builders, the Fred Harvey Company, in 1905. It is patterned after the great hunting lodges of Europe with a stone fireplace and mounted animals. ⚲ *South Rim • Map V2 • 303 297 2757 • $$$$*

Grand Canyon Lodge

The only hotel accommodation on the North Rim of the canyon, this lodge has cabins and a few modern motel rooms. Advance reservations are essential. ⚲ *Bright Angel Point • Map V2 • 303 297 2757 • www.grandcanyonlodge.com • $$$*

Grand Canyon Camper Village

With 250 RV hook-ups and 100 tent sites, this is one of the larger, privately run, year-round campgrounds. ⚲ *Grand Canyon Village • Map V2 • 928 638 2887 • $*

Zion Lodge

The complex includes 40 cabins with gas log fireplaces and private porches, and 75 motel rooms, each with two queen-size beds. ⚲ *Zion National Park • Map U1 • 435 772 3213 • $$$$*

Best Western Zion Park Inn

The inn is located at the foot of a 1,300-ft (430-m) cliff of Navajo sandstone. The 120 rooms are individually climate-controlled and some have kitchenettes. ⚲ *1215 Zion Park Blvd, Springdale • Map U1 • 800 934 7275, 435 772 3200 • $$$*

Cliffrose Lodge & Gardens, Zion

The setting is charming, with five acres of lawns, shade trees, and flower gardens along the Virgin River. Every room offers a spectacular view. ⚲ *281 Zion Park Blvd, Springdale • Map U1 • 435 772 3234 • $$$*

Furnace Creek Inn, Death Valley

Elegant and expensive, with glorious views of the Panamint Mountains. Guest rooms have quality furnishings. ⚲ *Furnace Creek • Map S1 • 760 786 2361 • $$$$$*

Furnace Creek Ranch, Death Valley

The rustic hostelry offers two spring-fed pools (the water is very warm), golf, tennis, and horseback riding. ⚲ *Furnace Creek • Map S1 • 760 786 2361 • $$$*

Stovepipe Wells Village, Death Valley

A bit off the beaten track, this is not a fancy place but has a pool, saloon, and general store. The nearby sand dunes are a photographer's delight. ⚲ *Stovepipe Wells • Map S2 • 760 786 2387 • $$$*

Note: *All hotels listed accept credit cards, have air conditioning, and rooms with private bathrooms*

Left **Hikers** Center left **Lake Mead marina** Center right **Sign on desert road**

Hiking Trails

1 Mouse's Tank, Valley of Fire

"Mouse" was the name of a Native American outlaw. The moderately easy, self-guiding trail to Mouse's Tank (a series of natural catchments) passes the best petroglyphs in the park.

2 Canyon Overlook Trail, Zion National Park

A moderate, short day-hike to the overlook, which is right above the Great Arch.

3 Observation Point – Hidden Canyon Trail, Zion

The 7.5-mile (12-km) round-trip hike is moderately difficult to Hidden Canyon, then strenuous to Observation Point, but the view from the point is the park's finest.

4 Riverside Walk, Zion

The paved walk at the base of a gorge is especially delightful in early October when the fall foliage is at its most beautiful.

5 Bright Angel Trail, Grand Canyon

The entire 19-mile (30-km) down-

Kilns, Wildrose Canyon

and-back round-trip descends 4,400 ft (1,342 m) and takes most hikers two days. Rest houses and a campground on the route.

6 Rim Trail, Grand Canyon

Extending from the Village area, the partially paved trail can be accessed at many points along Hermit Road and its terminus at Mather Point. Little elevation change and great views.

7 South Kaibab Trail, Grand Canyon

Access to the trailhead is by shuttle bus. The steep trail descends 4,500 ft (1,372 m), with no water along the down-and back 14-mile (22-km) route.

8 Wildrose Canyon to Wildrose Peak, Death Valley

A 4-mile (6-km) climb through woodland to the crest of the Panamint Mountains. Superb views.

9 Golden Canyon to Zabriskie Point, Death Valley

A low-elevation, 6-mile (9.5-km) round-trip hike featuring the finest badlands scenery in the monument, and traversing an area of fully exposed rock strata that represents millions of years.

10 Coffin Peak Trail, Death Valley

This easy trail starts at Dante's View, following a canyon into the Black Mountains. Vegetation is dominated by mormon tea, shadscale, and spiny desert shrubs.

Around the Region – Parks and Preserves

For park visitor information **See pp16–17, 99 & 102–103**

Left **All-terrain vehicle** Center **Start of scenic route** Right **Mountain biker**

🔟 Commercial Tours

1 Las Vegas Tour and Travel
The Indian Country Tour begins with a flight over Hoover Dam and Lake Mead, and continues to the Grand Canyon. Participants then take a bus tour along the canyon's rim. A barbecue lunch is included. ✆ *702 739 8975*

2 Papillon Grand Canyon Helicopters
The Grand Celebration Tour includes landing on the floor of the Grand Canyon, exploration of Native American lands, a champagne picnic, and views of Lake Mead, Hoover Dam, and the Las Vegas Strip. ✆ *702 736 7243*
• *www.papillon.com*

3 ATV Adventures
Open-air jeep tours through the Valley of Fire's back country to view wildlife, plants, and formations. Lunch and hotel pick-up are included. ✆ *800 519 2243, 702 398 7729* • *www.atv-jeep-tours.com*

4 Grand Canyon Railway Tour
Air Vegas offers an all-inclusive round-trip air fare to the Grand Canyon Railway. Board a vintage train and ride to the South Rim. A narrated motor bus tour and lunch are part of the package.
✆ *800 843 8724* • *www.airvegas.com*

5 Canyon Explorations
One of several companies providing hiking, interpretive trips, and whitewater rafting in the Grand Canyon. ✆ *928 774 4559*

6 ATV Wilderness Tours
Year-round guided trips in four-wheel all-terrain vehicles and jeeps. Three-hour to three-day outings are available. The company is based in St. George, Utah. ✆ *888 656 2887, 435 656 2887*
• *www.atvadventures.com*

7 Adventure Photo Tours
First stop on this 10-hour tour is the ghost town of Grafton, where segments of the movie *Butch Cassidy and the Sundance Kid* were filmed. Then it's on to the east entrance, the most spectacular entry way into Zion National Park. ✆ *702 889 8687*

8 Gray Line Tours/ Coach USA
The 7-hour Hoover Dam Discovery Tour includes a 90-minute ride aboard the *Desert Princess* paddlewheeler and a visit to Ethel M's Chocolate Factory. They also offer tours to the Grand Canyon. ✆ *1800 474 8134, 800 634 6579*

9 Travelocity
Hoover Dam day trips are offered, along with tours of the Grand Canyon and Red Rock Canyon. ✆ *800 634 6787, 702 597 5970*
• *www.showtickets.com*

10 Zion Ponderosa Ranch Resort
A number of guided activities, such as hiking, abseiling, mountain biking, and horseback riding in Zion National Park. ✆ *435 648 2700* • *www.zionponderosa.com*

STREETSMART

LAS VEGAS TOP 10

Left **Golfing holiday** Right **Summer sun**

☰10 What to Pack and When to Go

1 Rate Changes
Hotel rates skyrocket when the weather is best – from about mid-March through July and September until the first part of November. However, days can be close to perfect during February and November when rates are generally lower and there is less traffic and smaller crowds. Las Vegas Casino hotels offer lower rates on weekdays, with rates soaring at weekends and during conventions.

2 Tee-Timing
It's easier for golfers to get tee times during the winter months, March, and November. Although it can be windy, the temperature is usually comfortable for playing.

3 Consider Convention Dates
The three biggest annual conventions in Las Vegas, in November, April, and January, each attract well over 100,000 delegates. Do your utmost not to coincide with them: not only will room rates be at their highest, but traffic is heavy, and the lines waiting for restaurant service are daunting.

4 Daytime Wear
As far as clothes are concerned, just about anything goes. Although shorts and T-shirts are the uniform in very hot weather, you'll see people wearing everything from designer resort wear to

jeans and leather jackets the rest of the year. Bathing attire should be reserved for swimming pool areas. Women wear cover-ups and men generally wear shirts and shorts over their bathing suits when going between their rooms and the pool. Upscale hotels provide robes for guests' use.

5 After Dark Apparel
While comfort generally rules the dress code, some moderately priced restaurants have signs saying "No shoes, no shirts, no service." Sport coats (casual-styled jackets) are required at some of the more expensive restaurants, but neckties are not always a requisite. Most people dress up when going to production shows or nightclubs; Las Vegas residents tend to dress more formally (and flamboyantly) than visitors.

6 Health Matters
The sun shines an average of more than 300 days a year, so pack colored glasses, sunscreen, lip balm, moisturizer, and a hat.

7 Weather Wise
Keep in mind more than just the glorious sunshine: Las Vegas receives an average of only 4.21 inches of rainfall a year, with about half an inch falling during the wettest months, January and August. Humidity ranges from 14 percent to 41

percent. Winter is unpredictable: some days are very cold and windy, while others are warm enough for wearing shorts.

8 US Entry Requirements for Canadian Visitors
Canadians do need passports, and must show a photo I.D., such as a citizenship card, when entering the USA.

9 US Entry Requirements for Overseas Visitors
Citizens from Australia, New Zealand, Japan, Germany, France, the UK, and many other European countries can visit the USA for up to 90 days without a visa, so long as they have a valid passport. They will need to complete a Visa Waiver Form, usually on the incoming flight. Visitors from countries who do need a visa must apply to a US consulate or embassy, and may be asked for evidence of financial solvency and proof that they intend to return to their country of origin.

10 US Customs
Adult nonresidents are permitted to bring in a limited amount of duty-free goods. These include 0.2 gallons (1 liter) of alcohol, 200 cigarettes, 50 cigars (but not Cuban), and up to $100 worth of gifts. Cash amounts over $10,000 should be declared on entry.

Left **McCarran International Airport** Center **Car-rental agency** Right **Fly-drive option**

🔟 Arriving in Las Vegas

1 Air News
If you're among the 43 percent of Las Vegas visitors who fly to McCarran International Airport, check out the airport website for information and maps. The fifth busiest airport in the USA can be confusing when you don't know your way around.

2 Comparison Shopping
McCarran is served by all major US carriers and several international carriers, including Virgin Atlantic and British Airways, with both scheduled and charter flights. It's worth comparing prices thoroughly before making your reservation.

3 Fly-Drive and Gambling Deals
Fly-drive packages are a firm favorite with people on vacation in the USA. Investigate the so-called "Gamblers' Specials," too, which combine air travel and accommodation in Las Vegas.

4 Getting from the Airport to the City
The airport is 2.5 miles (4 km) south of the city center. Allow 10 minutes to travel by road between the airport and hotels on the Strip. Taxis, shuttles, and limousines wait outside the airport, and there are car rental agencies inside. The cheapest option is to take a bus: the CAT (Citizens Area Transit) bus routes 108 and 109 run between the airport, downtown, and the Strip.

5 Paying Fares
If you have forgotten to bring enough change for transportation between the airport and your hotel, cash machines (ATMs) are located throughout the airport, and these accept standard cards such as Visa, MasterCard, and American Express, as well as other major US cards.

6 Car Rental
If you are renting a car from the airport, be advised that the rental price may not include three taxes, which total 39.8 percent, charged on all airport car rentals. If you are in a hurry, use one of the rental agencies with counters at the airport, but bear in mind that agencies with off-site counters generally charge lower rates.

7 Car Rental Documents
Visitors who plan to rent a car must remember to bring along a valid driver's license and major credit card, both of which are required by all agencies. Drivers must also be at least 25 years old to rent a car. If your own automobile insurance does not cover rental vehicles, it is wise to buy the rental companies' own coverage.

Directory
Air News
www.mccarran.com

8 Road Rules
Visitors from abroad who plan to rent automobiles would be well advised to familiarize themselves with basic US driving rules and signage before they begin driving. Information is available at most vehicle-rental agencies.

9 Arriving by Road
If you are driving to Las Vegas from another part of the USA, you'll probably access the city either via I-15, which goes from Los Angeles to Salt Lake City, Utah, and beyond, or via I-95, which connects Washington, Oregon, Nevada, and Arizona. Try to avoid peak traffic times on these roads: arrive before 4pm or after 7pm.

10 Arriving by Train and Bus
Visitors who wish to travel to Las Vegas by train and bus can take the Amtrak Chief to Needles, California or Barstow, California, then transfer to the Amtrak bus service, which arrives at the Las Vegas Greyhound Station. For timetable and ticket information telephone 1800 872 7245 or visit www.amtrak.com.

➔ *For more on booking accommodations See p135*

Left **CAT (Citizen Area Transit) bus** Center **Local taxi** Right **Monorail**

Getting Around

1 Foot Power

Walking may well be the best way to travel the three-mile-long Strip: the sidewalks are wide and the terrain is flat. Since the city covers a large area, however, and is crisscrossed by multi-lane streets, you'll need a car or public transport-ation when visiting attractions in outlying areas.

2 Finding Your Routes

If you are going to be driving, procure a good map (the Rand McNally map, which can be obtained at supermar-kets, drugstores, and booksellers, is excellent). The city is laid out on a grid, with only a few principal thoroughfares running obliquely.

3 Traffic Talk

In town, be prepared for fast driving and heavy traffic. Avoid driving during rush hours (about 7–9 am and 4–7pm). Congestion on the Strip begins in late morning and continues until after midnight, especially on weekends from mid-March through October and when large special events take place. The city's major streets are six to eight lanes wide.

4 Parking Lots and Garages

Hotel/casinos on the Strip and in Glitter Gulch provide free parking in high-rise garages. Else-where they have huge parking lots and/or garages. Almost all hotels offer valet parking. When valet parking is full, preference is given to hotel guests over casino visitors.

5 On-street Parking

When parking on the street, be sure to read all posted signs about park-ing restrictions to avoid incurring fines or having your vehicle towed away. Fines for parking in disability-reserved spaces without a valid placard range from $100 to as much as $1,000.

6 Taxis

Hotel entrances on the Strip and downtown are the best places to find cabs. The standard fare includes an initial fee of $3.30, plus $2.20 for each additional mile, and about $0.20 a minute when stopped at a red light or stalled in traffic. In heavy traffic it can cost more than $20 to go from one end of the Strip to the other. Since taxi drivers know the city's less busy streets, a use-ful tip is to ask to be taken the quickest way rather than the shortest.

7 Trolleys, Trams, and Monorail

The exact fare of $2.50 is required for the trolley (8:30am–midnight daily), which stops at all major locations from the Strato-sphere in the north to Mandalay Bay in the south. Free trams con-nect TI with the Mirage and the Excalibur with Luxor and Mandalay Bay. The monorail operates along the Strip between MGM Grand and Sahara (8am–midnight daily). A one-ride ticket costs $5.

8 Public Transit System

The least expensive way to travel beyond down-town and the Strip is by CAT bus (Citizens Area Transit); CAT has an extensive network of routes. Fares are $2 on main tourist routes, $1.25 on others; seniors and children aged 6 to 17 pay $0.60).

9 Hotel Shuttles

You may have to pay for the shuttle service between the airport and some hotels, but others offer a free service to shopping areas and sight-seeing destinations.

10 Bike Riding

Bicycling along main arteries is not advised, but riding through resi-dential neighborhoods and at Red Rock Canyon can be very pleasurable. Bikes can be rented from various outlets; fees usually include helmets and water bottles.

Left **Strip trolley bus** Right **Vegas-style private tour vehicles**

🔟 Sources of Information

General Information

For overall information about the city, including accommodations, attractions, and shopping, contact the Las Vegas Convention & Visitors Authority (LVCVA).

Business Information

Visitors interested in business in the area can contact the Las Vegas Chamber of Commerce, which will direct them to the appropriate sources.

Directory

Citizens Area Transit
702 228 7433

Las Vegas Convention & Visitors Authority
3150 Paradise Rd • 702 892 0711 • www.visitlasvegas.com

Las Vegas Chamber of Commerce
3720 Howard Hughes Pkwy • 702 735 1616

Asian Chamber of Commerce
900 Karen Ave • 702 737 4300

Urban Chamber of Commerce
1048 W. Owens Ave • 702 648 6222

Latin Chamber of Commerce
300 N. 13th St • 702 385 7367

Las Vegas Advisor
3665 S. Procyon Ave • 702 252 0655

Ethnic Affairs

Information about Las Vegas's various ethnic businesses and attractions is available from such organizations as the Asian Chamber of Commerce, Black Chamber of Commerce, and Latin Chamber of Commerce.

Organization Information

If you belong to a worldwide organization such as Rotary International or would like to meet people with similar vocational interests or hobbies, your best source of information is an Internet search engine such as www.google.com or www.yahoo.com.

Magazine Information

For insights into places and people, pick up *Las Vegas Magazine*, also known as *LVM*. This weekly magazine *(right)* is aimed at visitors and is available at hotels. It contains feature articles as well as information on nightlife, shopping, gaming, and attractions.

Newspaper News

The *Las Vegas Review Journal* publishes dining and entertainment news throughout the week, as well as a "Best of Las Vegas" section once a year in March. You'll learn a lot by reading the ads, too!

Internet Info

For information on airlines, rental cars, and accommodations, use your favorite search engine to find websites with a Las Vegas focus. One of the most useful sites of the many available is www.visitlasvegas.com.

Cost Cutting

Bargain hunters will save money by subscribing to the *Las Vegas Advisor*. This monthly newsletter, aimed primarily at people who like to gamble, includes accommodation and dining deals that are also of use to non-gamblers.

Tourist Stations

The tourist stations along the Strip not only sell commercial tours, but they also have display racks containing promotional material about various attractions, which may be of use to you.

Out-of-Town Source

People traveling to Las Vegas via I-15 south manage to find special offers and deals that don't seem to be advertised anywhere else: the tourist information center in Jean, Nevada (near the border with California) has a reputation for handling the best Las Vegas coupons.

Streetsmart

Left **Bellagio's shopping arcade** Center **Las Vegas Outlet Center** Right **Pawnshop**

Shopping Tips

Shopping Arcades
Count on finding the most interesting upscale shopping in hotel arcades such as Miracle Mile at Planet Hollywood *(see p52)*, Bellagio's Via Bellagio *(see pp14–15)*, and Appian Way at Caesars Palace *(see pp26–7)*. All these are on Las Vegas Boulevard South, otherwise known as the Strip.

Malls
You have several choices for major mall-hopping. Boulevard, Meadows, and the Galleria at Sunset *(see p52)* are patronized primarily by locals, while tourists form the majority at two upscale malls on the Strip – the Forum Shops at Caesars *(see pp26–7)* and Fashion Show Mall *(see p52)*. The best sales at upscale shops such as Nieman Marcus and Saks Fifth Avenue (both at Fashion Show Mall) are held in January.

Bargain Buys
For bargains in high-quality merchandise, seek out the factory outlet centers. Las Vegas Outlet Center *(see pp53 & 91)* is just a few minutes

south of the Strip, while Fashion Outlet Las Vegas is near the California border at Primm. It is especially worth visiting these stores at the end of summer, when the merchandise is marked down even further.

Antiques
The city's greatest concentration of antiques stores is on East Charleston Boulevard, two miles or so from downtown. If you have time to visit only one cluster of stores, go to Antique Square (2014–2026 E. Charleston Boulevard), where a dozen different shops make up the complex.

Ethnic Shops
For the best authentic ethnic shopping, go to the stores that serve Las Vegas's various ethnic populations such as Asian Market (953 E. Sahara), Supermercado del Pueblo #2 (4972 S. Maryland Parkway), India Sweets & Spices (953 E. Sahara Avenue), Ethiopian Market (252 Convention Center Drive), and those in Chinatown Plaza *(see pp85 & 91)*.

Swap Meets
Swap meets, or flea markets, are usually held on Friday, Saturday, and Sunday, and are a great place to browse for bargains. The biggest meets are Fantastic

Indoor Swap Meet *(see p91)* and Broadacres Open Air Swap Meet (2960 Las Vegas Boulevard N.).

Pawn Shops
If you've never visited a pawn shop, Las Vegas is your chance. Much of the merchandise comes, of course, from gamblers in search of that little bit more money. The largest operation in town is Super-Pawn, with 18 outlets. A group of pawn shops are located in a street near Glitter Gulch *(see p80)*. If you want to make a purchase, don't agree to pay the first price you're quoted. Maybe not the second or third, either!

Business Hours
The larger malls and arcades are generally open 10am–9pm, seven days a week. Elsewhere stores may be closed on Sunday. Some of the Forum shops at Caesars stay open until midnight.

Taxes
Clark County levies an 8.2 percent "sales and use" tax on most goods. This is added to purchases at the cash register.

Credit Cards
Most businesses accept Visa and Master-Card. American Express, Diners, and other cards are not accepted as widely; travelers' checks in US dollars are accepted at many stores.

Left **Buffet restaurant** Center **The Convention Center** Right **Mirage Volcano**

🔟 Ways to Save Money

1 Planning Ahead
Start planning early – the best airfares may require three months' advance purchase.

2 Airline Deals from Other Parts of the USA
Combined air and hotel packages from most US cities to Las Vegas are especially good bargains. Keep in mind that airline fares to hub cities served by a number of carriers are almost always less expensive than routes on which there are few competing airlines.

3 Airline Deals from Other Countries
When Las Vegas is among two or more destinations you plan to visit in the USA, price each segment of your trip's airfare separately. Visitors from Europe, for example, often save money by buying round-trip tickets from their home country to New York or Chicago and then traveling in the USA by using a combination of one-way bargain air tickets and rental cars.

4 Timing
Time your trip to save money. Hotel rates change from day to day, based on supply and demand. They're most expensive on weekends, holidays, and during big conventions and important events. The less restricted your travel dates, the more money you can save: a room that costs $300 a night on a busy May weekend can go for $110 in November. Airfares are usually lower during the winter months, too.

5 Car Rentals
Car-rental rates change even more rapidly – sometimes hourly. Since rental reservations don't require a credit-card guarantee, lock in a reservation when you're quoted a good price. You can always cancel it later if you find a better deal.

6 Freebie Sources
When you arrive in the city, go directly to the information center run by the Las Vegas Convention & Visitors Authority *(see p115)*. Collect all the free magazines and brochures you can comfortably carry. Inside are coupons for special offers and money off shows and dinners, etc.

7 Meal Cost-Cutting
Eat your big meal of the day at noon. Lunch buffets usually cost a few dollars less than those offered at night, with virtually the same food served at both. If you're an early bird or a night owl, you'll save money on food: several casinos – notably those down-town and in outlying areas – offer low-cost meals between 11pm and 6 or 7am. These also work well for visitors affected by jet lag.

8 Discount Shopping
If you want to save money traveling to and from the shops, take bus 301 or 302 from the Strip and transfer to bus 303. You can also transfer to the free shuttle that goes to Las Vegas Outlet Center *(see pp53 & 91)*. The bus will cost a couple of dollars each way.

9 Entertainment Savings
The extravagant nightly light and sound shows and street performances at the Fremont Street Experience *(see p79)* are all free. Many of the big hotels along the Strip put on spectacular free shows to entice people in *(see p76)*. There are also less well-publicized free attractions such as the tropical bird display at the Tropicana Hotel and Casino. People-watching is entertaining, too *(see p77)*.

10 Free Special Events
Every so often, casinos put on promotions, bands present concerts, and organizations sponsor other free events. These are listed in the calendar sections of local papers and the various free entertainment magazines.

➤ *For more on free or low-cost entertainment* **See pp76 & 82**

Left *The Mirage* dolphin habitat Center *Excalibur* Right *Cirque du Soleil* at Bellagio

Types of Entertainment

1 Production Shows
Plan to see at least one production show (long-running show with spectacular production effects) while you're in town. A Las Vegas visit simply isn't complete without experiencing the excitement and professionalism of these top-notch performances. Although shows such as *"O"* and *Bette Midler* are expensive, others that cost less than half of their prices are also very well done.

2 Showtime
Most big shows go on twice nightly, with one or two nights off a week (varying from show to show). Daytime shows usually cost less.

3 Dining Options
Although most shows don't include meals or cocktails (there are refreshment stands outside most theaters), some hotels still feature dinner and cocktail shows. If you can, opt for the cocktail shows: they're less expensive. Moreover, the food at dinner shows doesn't tend to get rave reviews.

4 Other Shows
The production spectaculars aren't the only shows in town. Other long-running shows in hotel/casino theaters star magicians, comedians, and impersonators. Comedians on their way up also appear on Las Vegas comedy club stages.

5 Headliner Shows
If you're determined to see a particular entertainer perform in one of the city's famous headliner extravaganzas, order your tickets as soon as you hear about the performance. If you hesitate, you will probably still be able to buy tickets, but they will most likely be for the poorest seats in the priciest category. Las Vegas is a venue where top entertainers typically present just one performance; while the least expensive tickets may cost less than $100, top tickets can cost more than $1,000.

6 Lounge Shows
To stretch your entertainment dollars, take in a lounge show or two. You can watch some lounge acts for the price of a drink. Others are free.

7 Future Stars
If you like to know about the newest, most potentially hot acts, then go to see lots of lounge shows. Many of America's most celebrated entertainers – including Elvis Presley – appeared in Las Vegas casino lounges on their way to the top.

8 Chance Entertainment
In a town where entertainment is the name of the game, most Las Vegas visitors happen upon some unexpected treat during their visit. It may be a Dixieland band playing in a hotel plaza, a dance recital at a shopping center, a string quartet playing in a park, or strolling entertainers at the theme hotels.

9 Adults Only
Several clubs in the area around West Sahara Street south of downtown present adult-only entertainment. With names like Crazy Horse Saloon, Sapphire, and Palomino Club, they feature topless waitresses, amateur strip contests, and "beautiful friendly hostess dancers".

10 Culture
High culture doesn't necessarily come to mind when one thinks of Las Vegas. It is, in fact, the city's best-kept entertainment secret. Top-drawer artists from around the world perform regularly here: Luciano Pavarotti has sung at the Mandalay Bay; top orchestras and ballet troupes can be seen at the university. In addition, performers in the Las Vegas shows take part in actors equity, ballet, and musical productions when not in their regular roles.

For more about shows and entertainment See pp38–43

Left *Jubilee* Center *Le Rêve* Right *KÁ*

🔟 Tips on Buying Tickets

Advance Bookings
To avoid disappointment, order tickets for any production shows you want to see well in advance. You can do this either through your travel agent, by contacting the box office directly (when the production is at a hotel/casino theater, you can phone the hotel and your call will be transferred), or through a ticket agency such as Ticketmaster. It is almost impossible for ordinary tourists to buy tickets to the top shows such as *"O"* and *Mystère* on the day of the performance even if they are staying in the hotel where the show is playing.

Discount Tickets
Surplus same-day tickets for shows are sold at a discount at Tix4Tonight at Hawaiian Marketplace, outside Fashion Show Mall, opposite Echelon Resort, the Four Queens hotel, and near the giant Coke bottle north of MGM Grand.

Standby
When you want to see a show and can't get tickets in advance, you will increase your chances of getting standby seats by arriving early so you get one of the first places in line.

VIPs
If you're a high roller, you probably won't have to worry about standing in line at shows or anywhere else. Just let the VIP desk know what you would like to see.

Charting Your Course
When it is possible, ask to see the theater's seating chart. It's probably true that in the new theaters there isn't a bad seat in the house. Still, some seats are better than others, and as long as they all cost the same price, it is worthwhile choosing the ones you want.

Tipping
Tipping the *maître d'* or usher isn't always necessary. A growing number of theater tickets are issued electronically, and your seat is determined before you enter the theater. At theaters that have table-seating, however, guests are seated at the *maître d's* discretion. Palming him a $20 bill will usually get better seats, but do it in a discreet way.

University Venue Tickets
Tickets for performances at the Judy Bayley Theater or Artemis Hamm Concert Hall on the university campus can both be secured from the same box office; consult the Las Vegas Convention & Visitors Authority or local press for contact details.

Other Cultural Venues
Tickets for cultural programs presented at such venues as community arts centers and outdoor amphitheaters are usually, but not always, available from commercial ticket agencies including Ticketmaster. The yellow pages of the Las Vegas telephone directory list the numbers of various concert venue ticket offices.

Tour Group Tickets
People who are interested primarily in seeing Las Vegas shows should consult with their travel agents about tours that include them in their itineraries.

Ticket Information
If you have a problem finding ticket sources, try contacting the Las Vegas Convention & Visitors Authority *(see p115)*. Another good resource is the newsroom of the city's major newspapers.

Directory
Ticketmaster
702 474 4000

119

Left **Getting married at Bellagio** Center **Wedding chapel** Right **Elvis Presley's Vegas wedding**

Getting Married in Las Vegas

1 Getting a License

Marriage license requirements in Nevada have traditionally been less stringent than those in other parts of the USA. No blood tests are needed, nor is it necessary, after the license has been issued, to wait a set period before getting married. To obtain a marriage license, both partners must appear at the County Clerk's office in the Clark County Courthouse. Well over 100,000 weddings are performed in Clark County each year.

2 Identity Proof

Be prepared to produce your social security number and proof of identity such as a driver's license, certified copy of birth certificate, passport, or military ID. Divorced applicants need evidence that their divorces have been finalized, including date, city, and state where the decree was granted.

3 Age of Consent

People aged 18 years and older do not need consent to get married, but those aged between 16 and 18 must either have a consenting parent present or else produce a notorized document from a parent giving his or her consent.

4 Time-Saver

Couples planning a St Valentine's Day or New Year's Eve wedding should get their licenses well in advance to avoid long lines at the County Clerk's office.

5 Wedding Officiants

Nevada law requires that couples be married by civil marriage commissioners, justices of the peace, or bona fide ministers.

6 Civil Ceremonies

Civil marriages are performed one block from the Courthouse in the office of the Commissioner of Civil Marriages, for a fee of $50. One witness is required in addition to the person performing the ceremony.

7 Religious Rules

If your decision to have a religious wedding in Las Vegas is not a spur of the moment one, then have your usual minister, priest, or rabbi contact the head of the church or synagogue in Las Vegas where you want the ceremony to be held. That way you can resolve any discrepancies that may exist between different denominations regarding preparation for marriage, publication of banns, and the like.

8 Prices

You need $55 – in cash – for the license. Budget $75 for the use of a wedding chapel in a no-frills ceremony, $50 for the minister, plus any flowers, music, or costume rental. Weddings featuring an Elvis impersonator as minister start at $200. Make arrangements for a wedding-chapel ceremony in advance: they can't oblige drop-ins when fully booked.

9 Venues

With more than four dozen chapels, hundreds of churches, synagogues, public parks, ballrooms, and scenic spots, the number of wedding venues is limited only by the imagination; some officiants may be unwilling to perform skydiving or helicopter ceremonies!

10 Same-Sex Ceremonies

Same-sex marriages are not recognized in Nevada, but the Gay Chapel of Las Vegas, part of Viva Las Vegas Wedding Chapel *(See p50)*, performs commitment ceremonies.

Directory

Clark County Courthouse
201 S. 3rd St
• Open 8am–midnight daily
• 702 455 3156

Commissioner of Civil Marriages
309 S. 3rd St
• 8am–10pm daily

Gay Chapel of Las Vegas
1205 Las Vegas Blvd S.
• 800 574 4450

For the Top 10 wedding chapels **See pp50–51**

Left **Little Church of the West** Center **Wedding chapel** Right **Romantic Pamplemousse**

🔟 Honeymoon Packages

1 Hotel Packages
Since honeymoon packages are offered by virtually all of the hotels in Las Vegas, it definitely pays to shop around. The basic packages usually include an upgraded room, a bottle of champagne with souvenir champagne flutes, optional breakfast in bed, and dinner at one of the hotel's restaurants.

2 Seasonal Price Variations
Whereas wedding licenses cost $55 year-round and chapel fees remain fairly constant (St Valentine's Day and New Year's Eve being exceptions), honeymoon package prices are affected by the dates you choose. For example, a week-long honeymoon during the annual giant Comdex convention, with its 225,000 delegates, may well cost two to four times what it might during the preceeding or following week.

3 Bed-and-Breakfast Packages
If you fancy getting away from the crowds and bright lights, investigate bed-and-breakfast honeymoon packages and houseboat rentals *(See also page 134)*.

4 Internet Deals
Explore your options on the Internet. Each major hotel has a web-site, as do many of the smaller ones. Most of these include information on package deals.

5 Do-It-Yourself
You may feel that rather than opt for a lavish package you can make your honeymoon more special by doing it yourself, finding a regular hotel package and adding your own romantic touches – a box of Ethel M. gourmet chocolates (produced in Las Vegas), dining at an intimate restaurant such as Pamplemousse *(See p46)* and seeing the shows you choose.

6 Accommodation Advice
As far as accommodations are concerned, the general rule is that the further away you are from the Strip, the less expensive the rooms. There are, however, deluxe exceptions to the rule, such as the posh J. W. Marriott Las Vegas, The Palms, and the romantic Loews Lake Las Vegas *(See p37)*.

7 Professional Planning
Las Vegas Weddings has been arranging weddings and honeymoons in the city since 1973.

8 Trousseau Tip
Save some of your trousseau money for lingerie shopping in Las Vegas. The little nothings sold at places like Bare Essentials and A Slightly Sinful Adventure are definitely unusual!

9 Wedding Photos
For an inexpensive souvenir of your honey-moon, have your picture taken in costume at the photo concession in Excalibur, or have your faces put on a magazine cover at Cashman Photo in Miracle Mile at Planet Hollywood (702 792 3686).

10 Films
Honeymooners keen on the movies might find it fun to rent a copy of the 1991 Nicholas Cage comedy *Honeymoon in Vegas*, which is set in the city, to watch on the DVD in their honeymoon suite.

Directory

Bare Essentials
4029 W. Sahara Ave
• 702 247 4711

A Slightly Sinful Adventure
1232 Las Vegas Blvd S.
• 702 387 1006

General Information
www.vegas.com/weddings

Left **Sunset Station Casino sign** Right **Banks of slot machines**

🔟 Slot Clubs

Join Up
1 If you're planning to gamble, join a slot club. Almost every casino has one, which anyone over the age of 21 can join for free. These clubs give players various rewards in relation to the amount of gambling they do, whether they win or lose.

Maximizing Benefits
2 Compare clubs to determine which one has the prizes you like best and the most advantageous point system. For example, while the number of points required for similar rewards may be the same at two clubs, one of them may award two points for every five dollars that goes through a machine while the other requires only one dollar. You can join as many clubs as you like, but experts advise that you join only one so that you accumulate enough points to earn rewards.

Playing Cards
3 Insert your plastic membership card (issued upon registration) to get your points registered. When accumulated, these points can be exchanged for meals and discounts on rooms (or even free rooms), as well as logo items such as mugs, T-shirts, athletic bags, warm-up jackets, and caps. Some casinos offer cash rewards, too.

Slot-club Hosts
4 Almost every casino employs "slot-club hosts," who circulate around the casino. If you have questions about how to play various machines, ask them; ask, too, how long you have to play the machines to be "comped" for lunch, dinner, or entertainment in the casino's showroom (theater). This is accepted procedure, so don't be shy about asking.

Sign-up Savvy
5 Couples who are in Las Vegas for one trip should sign up together, since they will be issued two cards with points accumulated on the same account. Those who plan more trips to the area, however, will profit by signing up singly: casinos send offers such as a certain number of nights at reduced room rates; by signing up as individuals, the couple may be able to take advantage of twice as many nights at the reduced rate.

Payouts
6 Choose machines with the best payout schedules. These schedules are found on the front of each machine and indicate winning combinations and the value paid out when a combination is hit. As experienced machine players are aware, the video poker and slot machines in any given casino have varying payouts as well as payback ratios (the average percentage the machine pays back to the player).

Slot Club Money Management
7 Remember that in every casino game the house has the advantage (even the 100% and better return on the best-paying video poker machines is predicated upon perfect play). Losing $50 to earn a $6.95 buffet award is not a bargain.

Table Games
8 Many casinos include table games in their slot clubs. If you play table games at one of them, contact the pit boss to be sure your playing is included in the point count.

Cash-in Advice
9 Keep an eye on your watch when you plan to redeem your points. Many slot club booths close before midnight and don't open again until the next morning.

Future Plans
10 If you plan to return to Las Vegas quite soon, you might consider subscribing to the *Las Vegas Advisor*, which includes a monthly "Slot Club Update" column.

Left **Slot card** Right **Blackjack table**

🔟 Gaming Tournaments

1 Tournament Schedules

Gamblers should contact various casinos to determine if any gaming tournaments are planned for the time they will be in Las Vegas. These tournaments range from daily free events and those with low entry fees to four-day tournaments. Blackjack, slot machine, and video poker tourneys are the most popular.

2 Multi-Day Tournaments

Count on a good deal of free time during four-day tournaments, since actual play takes up only two or three hours. Entry fees usually include lodging (or rooms at reduced rates), some meals or food, and beverage credits for the entrant and a guest. Although entry fees may run into the thousands of dollars, typically they're in the $199 to $599 range. Prize money in the high-stakes tournaments can go as high as a million dollars.

3 Between Rounds

Keep in mind that the casinos' primary reason for putting on tournaments is their belief that participants will gamble in the casino during the time when they're not competing. Most regular slot or video-poker tournaments consist of three rounds of 20–30 minutes each at metered machines and require no money to be spent during tournament play. Winners of each round, as well as the players whose aggregate scores for the three rounds are highest, are awarded prizes.

4 Prizes

The amount of prize money varies, but the majority of tournaments award cash to a large percentage – perhaps a quarter – of the entrants.

5 Blackjack

If blackjack's your game, you'll find that tournaments generally consist of three rounds, with round winners advancing to semi-finals and finals. The entry fee usually covers a certain number of tourney chips, issued at the beginning of the tournament and again before the semi-final and final rounds.

6 High Rollers

If you're a high roller, be sure to get on the invitation list at your casinos of choice. Several casinos don't publicize their tournaments, but instead invite high-end players whose names have been selected from their databases. Complementary accommodations, food, and beverages are generally the properties' finest, and entry fees range all the way from zero to thousands of dollars.

7 Tourney Money Management

For people with finite resources, it is more practical to play in tournaments that have entry fees than those with no fee but participants play with their own money. At tournaments with unlimited buy-ins, players may pay additional money to buy more chips or machine play as the tournament progresses.

8 Playing Plus

When you're competing in a gaming tournament that depends on a combination of luck and skill, stay ahead of the game by sticking to soft drinks and bottled water, rather than complementary alcoholic drinks.

9 Tournament Machines

Don't expect the machines on the casino floor to hit winning combinations as often as the tournament machines. High scores and frequent jackpots create excitement, so as a rule the machines used in tournament play are set to produce lots of action.

10 Repeat Invitations

If you enjoy the gaming tournament experience and want to be invited again, send a thank-you note to the casino's special events director.

Left **Croupier setting a roulette table** Center **Baccarat** Right **Keno**

TOP 10 Gambling Tips

1 First and Foremost

Remember: gambling is a business. The house almost always wins. Think of it as an evening's entertainment, not as a way of making money. Decide in advance what you are willing to spend, and quit as soon as you have spent it. If you do win anything but want to keep playing then cash in frequently (put your original stake, plus part of your profit, aside) to come out ahead.

2 Casino Games

Blackjack (which is also called "21") is the table game at which players have the best odds. Other popular table games include craps (dice), baccarat, roulette, poker, and three games based on Five Card Stud poker: Caribbean Stud Poker, Let 'er Ride, and Pai Gow.

3 Slot Machines

Many experts believe that slot machines (slots) are addictive. They're the big money-earners for Nevada casinos. Some – video machines, particularly – involve an element of skill. Others are purely games of chance. Newer machines incorporate elements that make them more enticing than the traditional slots.

4 Money Matters

Inserting $10 or $20 bills into slot machine receptors (note that all machines are now coinless) allows for more rapid play, since players need only push a button and the selected amount of coins is deducted. When winning combinations are hit, payouts are added to the total rather than being ejected from the machine. Payouts are by ticket which guests cash at the casino cage.

5 Reading the Payout Tables

Many people who are new to slot machines don't realize that you aren't able to win the highest jackpots posted on a machine unless you insert the maximum number of coins the machine will accept. This means you have to decide whether you want to risk larger amounts, or would prefer to be disappointed if you hit the big one and don't have enough coins in to collect it.

6 Keno

Odds of winning at keno are the lowest of all casino games. The game is based on selecting certain numbers (from 1 to 80) that you hope will be among the 20 numbers to randomly appear. Payouts are based on the number of "catches" (matching numbers selected). Most casinos have keno lounges.

7 Gaming Terms

It is helpful to know at least some of the casino jargon. Hand pay: winnings paid by casino workers rather than machines. Stickman: a casino worker who uses a hook-shaped stick to move dice around a craps table. Shooter: the player whose turn it is to roll the dice. Tokes: tips given for services rendered. RFB comp: complimentary room, food, and beverages (usually given to customers who spend a lot). High roller: someone who wagers large amounts. Bust hand: in blackjack, a hand that totals more than 21.

8 Gaming Chips

Remember when gambling at the tables that chips are not "play money." At all Las Vegas casinos, $5 chips are red, $25 chips are green and $100 chips are black. The colors of higher denomination chips may vary.

9 Coupon Caution

Take advantage of casino two-for-one or other coupons only if you plan to gamble anyway. Don't let them take advantage of you by enticing you into gambling.

10 Hand Pays

When you hit a jackpot that is paid by casino personnel rather than the machine, it is customary to tip. Any amount is appreciated, but most people tip from three to five percent; big spenders may go as high as 10.

 For more on casinos and gambling See pp36–7 & 122–3

Left **Laying bets during a craps game** Center **Craps dice** Right **Arizona Charlie's casino**

TOP10 Gambling Risks

1 Forgetting to Take a Break

Don't gamble nonstop. Gambling can be mentally and physically exhausting. If you spend more than an hour deciding whether to hold 'em or fold 'em, or two hours hunched over a slot machine, gamblers' fatigue is bound to set in. Taking a break – perhaps a short stroll outside – will go a long way toward making you feel refreshed.

2 The "It's Due to Hit" Myth

Some gamblers have the idea that since a slot machine hasn't paid any jackpots for a long time, it's due. Not true. Each spin of the reels is an independent event and has nothing to do with what has gone before or will come after.

3 No Good at Math

Beware of penny multiple-coin machines. Casinos make more profit on these machines than on any others. While some machines have nine pay lines, most have 20 or 25. This means that for nine pay lines nine coins must be played if you want to gamble on all the possibilities, or multiples of up to 20 on other machines. As a result, you can bet up to $5 on one push of the deal button.

4 Not Keeping it to Yourself

Don't boast about your winnings anyplace where strangers might hear you. You never know who they might be – con artists or worse.

5 Free Drinks

Resist the cocktail waitresses who circulate throughout the casinos frequently passing out free drinks to gamblers. People who drink excessively don't play as well as they might and have even been know to leave winning tickets behind them when they go.

6 Air Pollution

If you don't like smoking, don't put up with smoke-filled rooms. Some casinos (usually the newer ones) have more effective mechanisms than others for getting rid of smoke. With so many casinos in the city, it isn't hard to find one of them.

7 Cashing Your Paycheck

All sorts of inducements – free drinks, free pulls on slot-machine handles, chances to enter drawings (prize draws) for cars and even houses – are offered so that people will cash their paychecks at casinos. Why? Because once a paycheck is cashed, it's easier to spend.

8 Neglecting to Set Yourself Limits

Don't neglect to set limits on the amount of money you can afford to lose. Conversely, it's not a good idea to set goals on how much you are going to win before you quit. Probabilities are that it will cost more than the goal itself to reach the goal. It's true that some people do win – at times enormous amounts. But the multi-million and billion-dollar hotel/casinos provide vivid proof that more money is lost than won.

9 Bad Deals

Resist the come-ons some casinos offer of $40 or even $100 in slot play for $20. Play is allowed only on specific machines, and it's only after paying their money that "suckers" learn the real rules.

10 Under-Age Gambling

Don't gamble unless you are 21 years or older. If apprehended, minors are either arrested or given a citation. In either case a court appearance will be required, as the offense is a misdemeanor and subject to penalties that can range from fines to community service or even jail sentences of up to one year.

Left **Excalibur** Center **Learning the ropes** Right **Palace Station**

Gaming Lessons

Player's Anxiety
To overcome new-player jitters, it's wise to take lessons in the games you want to play. These are usually available at the casinos listed Monday through Friday: they last about an hour and are free.

House Rules
Even if you play poker or baccarat regularly with friends, the benefit of lessons is that you will learn the procedures and protocols of casino play. Not knowing the rules can be embarrassing.

Timing
You'll get more out of gaming lessons if you take them in the morning. Casinos – the setting for most lessons – tend to be much noisier and distracting as the day wears on, which can make it difficult to concentrate on what the instructor is saying.

Tipping
Although there is no charge for the classes, your instructor will appreciate a tip. Any amount between $2 and $5 would be appropriate.

MGM Grand

A Winner
More than a half-dozen casinos on the Strip offer free gaming lessons. Among them are Excalibur, Circus Circus, Tropicana, and Imperial Palace. Class hours and the games taught vary from casino to casino.

Exotic Games
When you're ready to tackle Pai Gow, Caribbean Stud, and Let it Ride poker, phone Golden Nugget or The Palms for their lesson times.

Downtown Lessons
If you want to keep away from the Strip, then Binion's is one of the few downtown casinos that offers gaming lessons.

Off-Strip Instruction
Further afield – and a good choice if you have a car and don't want any parking hassles – Gold Coast Hotel and Casino is reputed to have good gaming instruction.

TV Classes
Instead of participating in group gaming lessons, guests at several hotels can learn how to play most casino games by watching the in-house programs on the TV sets in their rooms. Programs repeat at regular intervals throughout the day.

A Cautionary Note
So you've taken lessons. That doesn't mean you're an expert yet! Watch actual play before you start wagering, and then bet minimum amounts until you're experienced at casino play.

Blackjack

Directory of Casinos Offering Gaming Lessons

Binion's Gambling Hall & Hotel
128 Fremont St • 702 366 7397

Excalibur
3850 Las Vegas Blvd S. • 702 597 7777

Gold Coast Hotel & Casino
400 W. Flamingo Rd • 702 367 7111

Golden Nugget
129 Fremont St • 702 385 7111

Palms Casino Resort
4321 W. Flamingo Rd • 702 942 6961

Tropicana Resort & Casino
3801 Las Vegas Blvd S. • 702 739 2222

For more on casinos **See pp36–7**

Left **Wheelchair-access sign** Right **Monorail**

1 ADA Coordinators

Las Vegas is perhaps the world's most accessible city for people with disabilities. If you have any questions or any particular needs, have your travel agent contact the hotel's Americans with Disabilities Act (ADA) coordinator prior to your visit. Every major hotel-casino has one, responsible for ensuring that the facilities are accessible.

2 Airport Shuttles

Airport shuttles equipped with lifts are available at the airport baggage-claim area doors 1, 3, and 4. You may have to phone for a lift-equipped taxi, but direct-line phones are located in the baggage-claim area. Find out if car-rental company shuttles to their lots are lift-equipped, and let them know in advance if you need rear van seats removed and a ramp.

3 ADA Requirements

Bellagio, the Mirage, and Imperial Palace hotels have the reputation of being the best equipped for people with disabilities. All hotels, however, are supposed to have some rooms especially equipped for disabled guests. You may have to hunt around to find such specific amenities as roll-in showers, assisted-listening devices, vibrating alarm clocks, or televisions with telecaption devices.

4 Casino Accessibility

Every casino has accessible slot machines, and many have lowered tables with wheelchair access. Most bingo parlors have Braille and large-print game cards, and many casinos, if asked in advance, provide sign-language interpreters for gaming lessons.

5 Swimming Pools

Most hotels have lifts to assist guests into swimming pools; some of the pools with sand beaches also have wheelchair-accessible beach entrances.

6 Showroom Space

All Las Vegas venues for production and other shows (generally referred to as showrooms) have special areas for wheelchairs. Let personnel know in advance, since wheelchair users are often seated first.

7 Ramps and Restrooms

You can expect all public buildings, attractions, and hotel-casinos to be ramped and to have restrooms for the disabled. Curbs on most streets have been modified so that they are wheelchair accessible. City buses are fully accessible, as are some taxis, trams, shuttles, and the monorail. It is also possible to rent motorized carts (mechanized one-passenger carts used in lieu of wheelchairs).

8 Medication Schedules

If you need to take medication at certain times, wear a watch – there are no clocks in casinos.

9 Pedestrian Overcrossings

Don't worry about having to climb stairs at overhead pedestrian crossings. They can be reached by elevators or escalators.

10 Information

ADA coordinators may be able to answer your queries. Try the website listed below, too.

Directory

www.vegasdisability info.com

Bellagio

Left **Gay bookstore** Right **The city at night**

Gay and Lesbian Visitors

Acceptance
Opinions vary as to the degree of acceptance of gays and lesbians in Las Vegas. While the city is outwardly liberal and permissive – camp, even – its straight citizens are considered by some to be ultra-conservative in their views. Having said that, the city recently elected its first openly gay representative to the State Assembly. Many Las Vegas businesses, too, allow for what is euphemistically described as a "domestic partner" in their health-insurance plans.

Gay Organizations
There are more than 75 gay organizations active in Las Vegas, representing all sorts of interests, from singing to motorcycling.

Where the Action Is
The main gay section of Las Vegas, containing a number of gay bars and clubs, is in the Paradise Road, Harmon, and Tropicana avenues area, just east of the MGM Grand.

Clubs
If you feel at home with the younger crowd, head for Gipsy. Krave, the only gay bar on the strip, offers themed nights and cabaret. Flex puts on drag shows and wet T-shirt contests, while Snick's Place has become an icon, being the Las Vegas' oldest gay men's bar.

Transgender Bar
The Las Vegas Lounge is the city's only transgender bar.

Internet Information
You can get information about gay and lesbian venues in the city from several websites. Try www.gaynvegas.com for listings of accommodations and restaurants that are gay-owned or gay-friendly.

Meeting Venue
The Gay & Lesbian Community Center (known also just as The Center, *below*) sponsors frequent social events and is a venue for meetings of various gay and lesbian groups. It also offers free and confidential tests for HIV on Thursday afternoons from 1pm to 6pm.

Reading Material
Get Booked, the city's small but well-stocked gay bookstore, is open seven days a week.

Publications
For local gay-related news, pick up copies of the *Las Vegas Bugle* and *Out Las Vegas*. Both publications are available at local bars and at Get Booked bookstore.

Help Line
The organization PFLAG (Parents and Friends of Lesbians and Gays) runs a help-line, listed below.

Directory

Flex
4347 W. Charleston Road • 702 215 0669

The Gay & Lesbian Community Center
953 E. Sahara Avenue • 702 733 9800

Get Booked
4640 Paradise Rd • 702 737 7780 • Open 10am–midnight Mon–Thu, 10am–2am Fri–Sun

Gipsy
4605 Paradise Road • 702 731 1919

Krave
3663 Las Vegas Blvd S. • 702 836 0830

Las Vegas Lounge
900 E. Karen Ave • 702 737 9350

PFLAG Help Line
702 438 7838

Snick's Place
1402 S. Third Street • 702 385 9298

Websites
www.gayvegas.com
www.gaynvegas.com

Left **Bank of America sign** Center **ATM machine** Right **$50 bill**

📑10 Banking

Vegas Banking Hours
Most banks are open from 9am to either 5pm or 6pm Monday through Friday, and 9am–1pm on Saturday. Branches located in supermarkets tend to have longer hours and stay open all day on Saturday and sometimes on Sunday afternoon.

ATMs
Using ATM machines for cash and credit cards for purchases usually ensures the best exchange rates for foreign visitors. Be prepared to pay a fee, which will be charged to your account, for using an ATM at a bank that is not your own. Instructions for use should appear in English and Spanish, and sometimes Japanese.

Drive-Through Banking
For many simple money transactions, drive-through banking (often spelled "drive-thru" on signs) is the most convenient method. The windows are usually open for an additional half-hour at the beginning and end of the bank's regular business day. Drive-throughs usually have cash machines (ATMs), too.

Getting Hold of Cash
Check-cashing services, located at various places along the Strip and downtown, charge large fees, so it's best to try to use alternative methods of getting cash. Cash advances on credit cards are available from cash-advance machines at all hotel-casinos, but again the service will cost you: the typical fee is 5 percent (that's a $50 fee for cashing $1,000), with larger percentages for smaller amounts.

Cashing Personal Checks at Hotels
Most hotels will cash guests' personal checks, provided they are in US dollars. It is not general policy, however, to cash checks for non-guests.

Foreign Currency
Unlike banks in Europe, only a few Las Vegas banks handle foreign currency. Most convenient of these is probably Bank of America. Many hotel-casinos will exchange foreign currency from major countries, but they charge a fee in addition to the hotel's own exchange rate.

Traveler's Checks
Traveler's checks can be cashed at any bank or hotel-casino. Try to get the checks in US dollars to avoid paying an exchange fee each time you cash one; if you do use checks in a foreign currency, try to get large denominations to save on fees when you cash the checks.

US Currency Denominations
US bank notes come in denominations as low as $1 and as high as $1,000.

Dollar Bills
If you are unfamiliar with US banknotes, take heed of the fact that they are notoriously hard to differentiate; pay special attention to this when handing over money to taxi drivers etc. A $1 "bill" is just the same size and color as a $20.

Small Change
The US dollar (sometimes referred to as a "buck") is divided into 100 cents (called pennies). Coins come in one cent, five cent (nickel), ten cent (dime), 25 cent (quarter), and, less often, 50 cent (half-dollar) denominations.

Directory

Bank of America
6900 W. Cliff Drive
• 702 654 6512 • Open
9am–5pm Mon–Thu,
9am–6pm Fri, 9am–
1pm Sat • www.
bankofamerica.com

Left **Public Internet access** Center **Postage stamp** Right **Post Office sign**

🔟 Communications

1 Publications for Visitors

Useful entertainment guides include *What's On, Where, Today in Las Vegas, Monorail,* and *Las Vegas Magazine.* Look out for the discount coupons for meals or shows.

2 Las Vegas Newspapers

The city's principal newspapers, the *Las Vegas Review-Journal* and the *Las Vegas Sun,* are both published daily, the former in the morning and the latter in the afternoon.

3 Internet Access

A stay at a luxury hotel usually includes the cost of online usage in your room. If you require public Internet access, visit a local print shop such as Kinko's, which provides Internet access for a fee of \$0.20 a minute. Alternatively, for those with the time (and ambition), visit a local library and sign-up for a library card, which will allow you complimentary access for a preset amount of time.

4 Making Calls

To place a call within Las Vegas and environs, omit the 702 area code. When telephoning outside the area, you will need to dial a 1, followed by the appropriate area code and seven-digit number. Local calls cost 50 cents for three minutes. The easiest way to pay for long-distance calls is to insert your credit card. As elsewhere in the world, calls made from hotel rooms cost a great deal more than those made from pay phones.

5 Public Telephones

You'll find public telephones, or pay phones, outside supermarkets and gas stations, and in restaurants, hotels, and casinos all around the area. When they're inside buildings, phones are usually located near the restrooms.

Public phone

6 Cell Phones

If you want to rent a cell phone during your stay, consult the local yellow pages or have the hotel concierge locate one for you.

7 Hotel Business Centers

Most major hotels have business centers for guests' use (although not for free) equipped with the latest computers; some also offer secretarial services and have guest rooms equipped with "dataports" for computers, fax, and internet usage.

8 Western Union

If you need to send international telegrams, ask hotel personnel where to find the nearest Western Union office. You can also use Western Union for wiring funds.

9 Post Offices

You can have incoming mail sent either direct to your hotel or to "General Delivery" at any US Post Office in the city. Two post offices that are conveniently located for visitors are the Downtown Station and the General Mail Facility.

10 TV and Radio

Choose from around 40 local radio and TV stations. If the local fare fails to satisfy, your hotel is very likely to have cable or satellite TV.

Directory

Cyber Stop Internet Café
3743 Las Vegas Blvd S.
702 736 4782

Kinko's Downtown
830 S. 4th St
702 383 7022

US Post Office Downtown
301 Stewart Ave
• Open 9am–5pm
Mon–Fri, 9am–1pm Sat

US Post Office
1001 E. Sunset Rd
• Open 6:30am–10pm
Mon–Fri, 8am–4pm Sat

Left **Security guard** Right **Police car**

🔟 Things to Avoid

1 Traffic Tangle
Any street intersecting with Las Vegas Boulevard South means slow traffic, but drivers should avoid the Tropicana–Las Vegas Boulevard intersection altogether, if possible: it is the busiest intersection in the city and can take 15 minutes or more to get through.

2 Crime Zone
Although the Strip and the five-block Fremont Street Experience pedestrian mall are considered safe at any time, certain areas in North Las Vegas and on S. Maryland Parkway, around Sunrise Hospital, are not. The area north of Las Vegas library on Las Vegas Boulevard North is perhaps the roughest neighborhood in town. Do not walk there.

3 Con Artists
Rings of confidence tricksters – men and women – frequently operate in Nevada, with all sorts of scams. They prey primarily, but not exclusively, on the elderly. Beware anyone who approaches you with an offer that seems too good to be true, and never agree to collect jackpot winnings for another person on the promise that you'll be paid for doing so. Card sharps in particular look for suckers. Don't be one: if a deals sounds too good to be true, it probably is.

4 Resist the Girlie Clubs
Men are lured inside with bold promises, persuaded to pay extraordinary amounts for watered-down drinks, then sent on their way, not necessarily with the promised sexual favors. Prostitution is legal in the state of Nevada except in five counties, including Clark County. Las Vegas is in Clark County, so apprehended prostitutes and their customers are subject to fines and imprisonment.

5 Cache Your Cash
Don't wear expensive jewelry: it alerts robbers or pickpockets to the fact that you would be a lucrative target. Keep valuables in your room safe if there is one, or in the hotel's safe if there isn't. Keep your belongings with you at all times: the excitement of the bright lights, music, and carnival atmosphere can be distracting. If you win a large amount of money, ask for it in the form of a check rather than cash. Casinos will also provide security escorts for customers who request them.

6 Don't Let the Kids Roam
Do not allow youngsters under the age of 16 to go out on their own; children under 12 should not go without adults to malls or game arcades, even if they are in a group.

7 Car Trouble
Avoid poorly lighted garages and parking lots at night, especially when they seem deserted. Lock your car doors even when you are driving. Put all packages and luggage in the trunk. When you leave your car at valet parking, it's wise to remove anything of value and have only your car and trunk keys on the key-ring.

8 Mealtime Precautions
Cold soup and warm potato salad are potential sources of food poisoning, so when eating at buffets make sure that the food that is supposed to be hot is hot, and the food that is supposed to be cold is cold.

9 Panhandlers
It's up to you, of course, whether you give money to panhandlers (beggars), but you might consider contributing instead to charities that provide food and shelter for the homeless.

10 Law-Enforcement Officers
Despite the carefree atmosphere of Las Vegas, the police department is strict about enforcing the city's laws. Don't do anything here that you wouldn't do in your own home town.

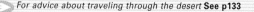

For advice about traveling through the desert **See p133**

Left **Desert sign** Center **Temperature gauge** Right **Drugstore sign**

Ways to Stay Healthy

1 Becoming Acclimated
Give your body a chance to become acclimated upon arrival before engaging in strenuous activity, especially if you have traveled a long distance or from a much different climate or altitude. Because of the dry weather, for example, people prone to nosebleeds may experience problems.

2 Taking the Water
Nevada's low humidity means that you must drink plenty of fluids each day (alcoholic beverages don't count), especially during the summer. Dehydration and heat stroke account for many emergency medical service calls.

3 Solar Protection
Slather on the sunscreen whenever you go outdoors, not just when at the hotel pool. Even when the Nevada sunlight is filtered through clouds, it can burn.

4 Precautionary Measures
Pollution caused by blowing desert dust, vehicle emissions, and microscopic grit from construction sites can be a problem for people with respiratory problems.

5 Allergies and Arthritis
People with allergies to dust and sagebrush may have a problem in Las Vegas. However, most people with arthritis find that the low humidity is more comfortable for them than climates with higher humidity.

6 Overindulgence
Drinking too much is easy in the casinos' party atmosphere of bright lights and free drinks. It's up to you how much you indulge, but do not even think about driving afterward. Under Nevada law, the blood alcohol level at which a person is presumed intoxicated is 0.1 percent and can bring about a court appearance and heavy fine if the driver is stopped by police. In the case of an accident involving fatalities, it can result in imprisonment.

7 Insurance
Travel insurance may not be mandatory for visitors to the USA, but it is emphatically recommended because emergency medical and dental care can be extremely expensive. In most cases, people incurring medical expenses are required to make payment (or arrangement for it) before leaving the clinic, hospital, or physician's office.

8 Take Your Medicine
Remember that there are no clocks in casinos: the excitement of gaming may make you forget to take your regular medications. (Also be aware of those that shouldn't be taken with alcohol.) To have prescriptions filled, go either to drugstores (pharmacies) or the pharmacy departments of supermarkets, several of which are open 24 hours.

9 In Case of Illness
Since Las Vegas has more tourists than any other US destination, the medical professional is especially mindful of the need for in-room service (not usual in the USA). If you develop a condition that requires medical attention, Inn-House Doctor, Inc. offers free telephone consultations and the doctors make hotel visits if necessary. Harmon Medical Center offers a walk-in clinic and is open 24 hours daily; you will need medical insurance and some ID to use this service. House Call Physicians specializes in in-room care for most types of medical problems.

10 Medical Emergencies
In case of an extreme medical emergency, dial 911 from any telephone (remember to dial the appropriate number to get an outside line if you're in your hotel room or dial "0" and ask the operator to dial it for you and send help to your room immediately.

Above **A desert walk just after sunrise, before ground temperatures rise**

🔟 Desert Precautions

Water Requirements
Be sure to carry drinking water. A gallon per person per day is suggested. The outdoor enthusiasts' greatest dangers are from hypothermia (extreme over-cooling) and heatstroke (extreme over-heating). Preventing dehydration helps avoid the latter. Carry water for your car, too. Even the radiators of new cars can overheat when outside temperatures hit 120°F (nearly 50°C).

Car Check
Be sure your car is in good mechanical condition and that it has a full gas tank. Stay on paved roads; do not drive on the shoulder, if possible, because there is danger of being trapped in the sand.

Flash Floods
Don't try to drive through flooded areas. If water begins to rise over the road, it is actually best to abandon your car and move to high ground.

Don't Go Solo
Never venture into the desert alone, and don't go hiking without a map and a good compass, even if you have a Global Positioning System (GPS).

Tell Somebody
Whenever you go hiking in the desert, advise a park ranger or other responsible person of your destination and estimated time of return. In case you become lost, search and rescue teams can work more effectively if they have information to guide them.

Dress Properly
Layered clothing slows dehydration and minimizes exposure. Summer temperatures up to 125°F (52°C). are not uncommon, and winter temperatures can plunge below freezing. During the course of a typical day and night, there may be a huge variation in temperature.

Be Prepared
Always carry a first-aid kit when hiking. Every hiker over the age of 12 should know CPR and basic first aid.

Dangerous Creatures
Beware of rattlesnakes and scorpions. Before you go, learn how to treat their bites (getting medical help as quickly as possible is recommended). Other dangerous animals and insects that live in the desert are gila monsters, mountain lions, wild boar, bears, killer bees, and centipedes. Wildlife may seem tame but will attack if they feel threatened or that their young are in danger.

Cover Your Head
Wear a hat to help prevent heatstroke whenever you are subjected to the desert sun's rays in the middle of the day – even when it is overcast. Even if you spend only minutes outside, you should protect your skin with sunscreen and use lip balm. Moisturizer is helpful in the desert climate as well.

Curb Your Curiousity
Stay away from abandoned mines. They are very dangerous because of the possibility of cave-ins, sharp drop-offs, and deadly gases.

Directory

Emergency Number
911

Inn-House Doctor, Inc
702 259 1616

Harmon Medical Center
150 E. Harmon Ave •
Map Q3 • 702 796 1116

House-Call Doctor
1515 E. Tropicana Ave
• 702 474 6300

Left **Wigwam** Center **RV Parking lot entrance, Laughlin** Right **Tent in a national park**

TOP 10 Camping and Houseboating

1 Research your Campsites

Camping in city parks is generally not permitted. Camping in state and national parks is permitted in spaces designated for that use, and some off-trail overnight camping for hikers is allowed. Most state and national park and recreation area campgrounds have a first come, first served policy, so arrive early to have a better chance of getting a site. However, since other campgrounds require reservations, you'll need to contact them in advance. Be sure to obey all campground rules regarding fires, keeping pets on a leash, and the disposal of trash.

2 Tent Sites

There are only 15 tent sites at Red Rock Canyon but if you are lucky enough to find one free you can stay up to 14 days. There are also tent sites at Mt. Charleston and campsites around Lake Mead.

3 Reservations

Make reservations at privately owned campgrounds as far in advance as possible. As camping increases in popularity, it is more difficult to get a space without reservations. This is especially true during the summer when schoolchildren are on vacation and in the early autumn, a favorite holiday time for seniors.

4 Casino Campgrounds

It's especially important to reserve early if you want to stay at one of the casino camping facilities. Circusland RV Park is adjacent to Circus Circus on the Strip, and Sam's Town RV Park is near Sam's Town Hotel & Gambling Hall.

5 RV-Friendly Parking Lots

Laughlin is the most RV-friendly area in southern Nevada. Recreational vehicles can be parked in its casino parking lots overnight and there are several recreational vehicle parks on the other side of the Colorado River in Bullhead City, Arizona.

6 RV Rentals

If you would like to rent a recreational vehicle while you're in Las Vegas, you can choose from more than half a dozen rental companies. You will find them listed in the yellow pages of the Las Vegas telephone directory and on the Internet.

7 Campground Caution

Never camp in or near a dry wash (the course water takes when it rains) because of the potential for flash floods. Do not camp on the top of a large hill because of the danger from lightning and extreme winds.

8 Downpours

If you are camping in the desert when heavy rains begin, move to high ground immediately – at least 30 to 40 ft (10 m) above the canyon floor or bottom of a dry wash is recommended.

9 Houseboating

To rent a houseboat, contact either Seven Crown Resorts or Forever Resorts well in advance. The Forever Resorts marina at Callville Bay, the closer of the two, is about a 45-minute drive from the Las Vegas Strip.

10 Season Selection

Summer may be unpleasantly hot but is the peak season for campers and houseboaters: make arrangements up to a year in advance. The best rental values are during the winter, but the weather may not be pleasant. Consider renting a houseboat either during spring or fall.

Directory

Circusland RV Park
500 Circus Circus Drive • 800 634 3450

Sam's Town RV Park
4040 S. Nellis Blvd • 702 454 8055

Seven Crown Resorts
800 752 9669 • www. sevencrown.com

Forever Resorts
800 255 5561

Left **Mule riding** Center **Luxury hotel interior** Right **New Year celebrations, the Strip**

TOP 10 Tips on Booking a Hotel

1 Choose an Appropiate Hotel

Take your personal travel style into consideration when choosing where to stay. If you like action and don't mind noise, you will want to stay on the Strip or downtown. If gaming will play only a minor part in your holiday, you will be better off staying at a hostelry that doesn't have a casino.

2 Travel Agents

The easiest way to reserve Las Vegas rooms is by having a travel agent book them for you. However, travel agents often do not have access to money-saving resources or time to access them.

3 Arrangements on the Internet

Almost all major Las Vegas hotel/casinos have their own Web sites on which they offer online bookings and advertise promotions. These are listed under their main entries within this book.

4 Packages

Explore the many airline/ accommodations packages. The least expensive of these are gambling junkets that usually include airline flights and two- to four-night hotel stays, based on double occupancy. There are often, but not always, several hotel choices in various price categories.

5 Individual Requirements

To make the most satisfactory room arrangements, phone the hotel directly to talk with a reservationist. By discussing your needs with a person who knows the hotel intimately you are more likely to get exactly the room that you want.

6 Bargains

For rock-bottom Las Vegas room rates, time your stay to coincide with the days preceding and following New Year's Eve and New Year's Day (or the entire weekend if New Year falls within one), as well as the days between the National Finals Rodeo and Christmas. Hotel websites are usually the best places to find special deals throughout the year.

7 Times to Avoid

Room rates are usually higher over weekends and can more than quadruple when there is a major convention at the hotel or nearby *(see p117)*.

8 National Parks

National parks in the USA have become extremely popular in recent years – especially those in the American southwest. The effect of this is that booking accommodations within the parks, as well as whitewater rafting and mule rides at Grand Canyon should be made at least a year in advance. Otherwise, you will have to stay in an outlying area.

9 Outlying Areas

Accommodations in Laughlin, Boulder City, Mesquite, and areas within the Las Vegas orbit are not as difficult to obtain nor as expensive as most of those in Las Vegas or Henderson.

10 Last-Minute Rates

If you are extremely flexible, you can take advantage of last-minute cancellations even when the city is at its most crowded by calling the Las Vegas Convention & Visitors Authority *(see p115)*.

Houseboats in the Seven Crown Resort

Index

Page numbers in **bold** type refer to main entries.

Acknowledgements

ALAMY IMAGES: Gistimages 75tc.

Courtesy of THE BELLAGIO: Russell MacMasters Photography 2tl, 14b, 15c, 31br, 46b, 50c, 77c, 120tl; THE BLUE MAN GROUP: Ken Howard 38tr; BUREAU OF RECLAMATION: Andrew Pernick 92t.

Courtesy of CAESARS PALACE: 64tr; 74tl, 76tr; PURE nightclub 42tr; courtesy of THE CENTER: 128b; CHINOIS: 47ca; CIRQUE DU SOLEIL: Photos by Tomas Muscionico Costumes Marie-Chantale Vaillancourt 38tc, 119tr, Photo Veronique Vial Costumes Dominique Lemieux 38c, 119c; © Al Seib 38b; CORBIS: Bettmann 30c, 31t, 120tr; Richard Cummins 50tr.

Courtesy THE DESERT INN: 135tc.

Courtesy of EXCALIBUR: 135tr. THE FIRM PUBLIC RELATIONS & MARKETING: 13tr; courtesy of THE FORUM SHOPS: 26t, 26b.

Courtesy of GET BOOKED: 128tl.

Courtesy of HARRAH'S: 36tr; HULTON ARCHIVE: Archive Pictures 30c.

Courtesy of JUBILEE: 3tcl, 39t, 119tl; JW MARRIOTT LAS VEGAS RESORT & SPA: 88tl.

LAS VEGAS CONVENTION & VISITORS AUTHORITY: 56tl, 66cla; courtesy of LAS VEGAS HILTON: 56c; LAS VEGAS MAGAZINE: 115cb; LAS VEGAS SUN: Lori Cain 58tr; Steve Marcus 58b; Aaron Mayes 85, 87tr; Sam Morris 59t, 86b; Ethan Miller 84tr, 87cb; Marsh Starks 58tl, 59b.

Courtesy of MANDALAY BAY: 43t, 112tr; courtesy of the MGM GRAND: 42tl, 42b, 46tc, 126b, 128tr; MGM MIRAGE: 36cb, 42tc, 47tr, 52br, 64bl, 65tr, 77tr, 117tr, 118tc, 118tl, 118tr; courtesy of THE MIRAGE 46tc, 64tl, 66b, 73b, 117tr. N9NEGROUP: 42c; NHPA: David Middleton 104c.

THE RAINBOW COMPANY YOUTH THEATER: Tom Dyer 66tr; RIO SUITE HOTEL: 87bl.

STONE: Stewart Cohen 6t, 8–9; Kerrick James 110–11; Jake Rajs 6bl, 12, 80t; courtesy of STRATOSPHERE TOWER: 56b.

Courtesy of TI 76tl; TOWN SQUARE LAS VEGAS: 53c; courtesy of TROPICANA RESORT AND CASINO: 38tl.

Courtesy of THE VENETIAN: 20t, 32tl, 71t.

Courtesy of WYNN LAS VEGAS: Scott Forest 23tr, Robert Miller 7cb, 22cla, 22–23, 23cr, Tomasz Rossa 22bc, 119tr.

Pull out map cover – DK IMAGES: Rough Guides/Demetrio Carrasco.

All other images are © Dorling Kindersley. For further information see *www.dkimages.com*

Acknowledgements

The Author
Connie Emerson, who has lived in Nevada for more than 30 years, writes travel articles for national and international publications.

Produced by Blue Island Publishing, Highbury, London

Editorial Director
Rosalyn Thiro

Art Director
Stephen Bere

Editors
Michael Ellis
Charlotte Rundall

Designers
Tony Foo
Ian Midson

Picture Research
Ellen Root

Research Assistance
Amaia Allende
Emma Wilson

Main Photographer
Demetrio Carrasco

Other Photographers
Nigel Hicks
Alan Keohane
Tim Ridley
Greg Ward

Artwork
Chris Orr & Associates

Proofreader
Stephanie Driver

Index
Hilary Bird

AT DORLING KINDERSLEY:
Director of Publishing
Gillian Allan

Senior Publishing Manager
Louise Bostock Lang

Publishing Manager
Kate Poole

Senior Art Editor
Marisa Renzullo

Cartography Co-ordinator
Casper Morris

DTP
Jason Little

Production
Sarah Dodd, Marie Ingledew

Cartography
John Plumer

Additional editorial and design assistance
Emma Anacootee, Karen Constanti, Connie Emerson, Mariana Evmolpidou, Anna Freiberger, Rhiannon Furbear, Jo Gardner, Eric Grossman, Rebecca Ingram Frisch, Claire Jones, Sam Merrell, Collette Sadler, AnneLise Sorensen, Karen Villabona, Ros Walford

Dorling Kindersley would like to thank all the hotels, restaurants, shops, museums, galleries, and other sights for their assistance and kind permission to photograph at their establishments.

Placement Key: t = top; tl–top left; tr–top right; c–center; cb–center below; b–bottom; bl–bottom left; br–bottom right; l–left; d–detail.